BORN TO GLOW

The VEGAS GOLDEN KNIGHTS' Historic Inaugural Season

T0096065

Las Vegas Sun

Copyright © 2018 Las Vegas Sun

No part of this publication may be reproduced, stored in a retrieval system or transmitted in any form by any means, electronic, mechanical, photocopying or otherwise, without prior written permission of the publisher, Triumph Books LLC, 814 North Franklin Street; Chicago, Illinois 60610.

This book is available in quantity at special discounts for your group or organization.
For further information, contact:

Triumph Books LLC
814 North Franklin Street
Chicago, Illinois 60610
Phone: (312) 337-0747
www.triumphbooks.com

Printed in U.S.A.
ISBN: 9781629375595

Las Vegas Sun
Hank Greenspun, Founder, Publisher & Editor (1950 - 1989)
Barbara Greenspun, Publisher (1989 - 2010)
Mike O'Callaghan, Executive Editor (1979 – 2004)

Brian Greenspun
CEO, Publisher and Editor

Robert Cauthorn, Chief Operating Officer
Ray Brewer, Managing Editor
Case Keefer, Assistant Sports Editor
Jesse Granger, Reporter
Wade McAferty, Night Editor
Yasmina Chavez, Steve Marcus, Wade Vandervort, Photographer
Mike Smith, Editorial Cartoonist

Content packaged by Mojo Media, Inc.
Jason Hinman: Creative Director
Joe Funk: Editor

Front cover photo by AP Images. Back cover photo by Las Vegas Sun.
Cover Design: Preston Pisellini

Las Vegas Sun

CONTENTS

INTRODUCTION

Golden Knights' Season Defined by Bond They Formed With Las Vegas

By Jesse Granger • June 7, 2018

This isn't how this was supposed to end.

The Golden Knights' storybook season turned its final page Thursday night at T-Mobile Arena, with the players standing in shock at their blue line, staring down the rink as the Washington Capitals dogpiled in celebration after winning the first Stanley Cup in their 44-year franchise history.

"It's the worst feeling ever," Golden Knights defenseman Deryk Engelland said. "You never want to lose any game, but at this point it's awful."

But what will define this season is what happened next.

Each player tapped their stick on the ice and raised it high above their heads as a final salute to the fans. Thousands of steel gray and gold-clad faithful rose to their feet and cheered on their Knights — the first major professional team many of them have ever had to call their own.

It was far and away the single greatest inaugural season by an expansion team in sports history, but it's tough to decide which was more surprising — the Golden Knights' results on the ice or the way a city in the middle of the desert rallied around them.

In all its history, Las Vegas has been defined by a 4.2-mile stretch of road and all the gambling, partying and various trappings. Nearly 500 commercial planes fly into McCarran International Airport every day, and they almost always end their flight with a joke from the captain along the lines of "Welcome to lost wages," or another corny joke about the Strip.

But a recent flight from Winnipeg during the Western Conference finals series ended with an announcement saying, "Welcome to Las Vegas, home of our Golden Knights," and elicited a cabin full of cheers.

The key word is "our."

It's not to discredit UNLV basketball and the amazing runs it made, but as a college there are factions of Las Vegans that don't identify with the Runnin' Rebels. For the first time ever, native Las Vegans had something beyond the tourist attractions to represent them. Something to be proud of.

The Golden Knights may have better teams than this one. It was, after all, their first season. But this group of players and the bond they formed with the city will never be matched.

It started on Oct. 1, when a gunman opened fire on a crowd of concertgoers at the Route 91 Harvest music festival in what would be the deadliest mass shooting by an individual in modern U.S. history.

Only hours after the shooting, players who hadn't lived in Las Vegas for more than several weeks immediately asked what they could do. They visited first responders at the Metro Police station, stood in line with volunteers at food banks and met with victims.

"(I'm most proud of) the group in here," Engelland said. "Coming together as quick as they could and getting

into the community after a horrible tragedy, and going on a run. We came up a little short."

The players treated Las Vegas as their home, and the fans immediately latched on.

"It was seriously an amazing experience," Jonathan Marchessault said. "I've never felt part of a family like this. The community was unbelievable and the fans were amazing. I've never wanted to go to war more with a bunch of guys and it's been fun."

During preseason training camp, the red bleachers at City National Arena were usually empty. That changed quickly, as fans started packing the facility so full that the team had to place restrictions on practice attendance for safety concerns.

Many doubted the Golden Knights as a hockey team,

and they proved them wrong to the tune of 51 regular-season wins, a Pacific Division crown and a Western Conference championship.

"No one gave us a chance at all from the start," David Perron said. "I don't think anyone believed it when we were doing interviews over the summer, getting picked by Vegas. It's going to be a fun experience but not much else, and it was one heck of a ride."

Las Vegas as a hockey market was similarly doubted, but the fans sold out T-Mobile Arena for every single home game, set new records for ticket prices in the playoffs, and wrapped lines around the building, waiting hours for a chance to see the team run a 20-minute morning skate.

The players brought the Stanley Cup Final to Las

Vegas with their play, and the city showed it belonged. T-Mobile Arena arguably provided the best home-ice advantage in the NHL, especially in the playoffs. The 18,000-plus fans screaming at the top of their lungs and waving battle towels above their heads made Las Vegas a nightmare for opposing teams all season long, but eventually the Capitals solved the Golden Knights' riddle.

"It's difficult to come up short," a glassy-eyed Alex Tuch said, fighting back his emotions in the locker room after the game. "I had the time of my life, but it wouldn't be the same without this group of guys."

The heartbreak Tuch and his teammates felt Thursday night as they watched Alex Ovechkin and the rest of the Washington Capitals lift the Stanley Cup is probably similar to the thousands of fans around the valley whose emotions swung on every pass, save and goal.

"Thank you for all the support throughout the season," goaltender Marc-Andre Fleury said, as his message to the fans. "From Day One they've been incredible. I'm sorry we couldn't bring it home."

Fleury has no need to be sorry. The Golden Knights didn't deliver a championship, but they gave Las Vegans something better.

For many heartbroken Golden Knights fans, this is the first time they've ever had a home team to care this much for. The Golden Knights offered a distraction after the worst tragedy in Las Vegas history, they provided regular fixes of euphoria during their run to the Stanley Cup Final, and in the end, they provided the heartache that inevitably accompanies having a team to care about.

"At the end of the day, we had a taste of it," Marchessault said. "You don't want to finish on a note like that necessarily, and one thing I know is we'll be back." ∎

Accompanied by Vegas Golden Knights mascot Chance, a knight poses for the camera during a parade preceding Game 3 of the Western Conference Finals. (Las Vegas Sun)

Las Vegas Sun

DAWN IN THE DESERT

Vegas Golden Knights Fans Make Presence Felt at NHL Awards

By Ray Brewer • June 21, 2017

Los Angeles Kings fans were asked to stand and cheer. Instead, an emphatic chorus of boos exploded inside the T-Mobile Arena in Las Vegas.

Next, the public address announcer asked how many San Jose Sharks fans were in attendance for tonight's NHL Awards. There was absolute silence.

"How about the Vegas Golden Knights?" she then asked. The fans in the building, many sporting black and gold Golden Knights gear, went wild.

What a moment in our town's sports existence. No longer are Southern Nevadans forced to root for regional franchises like the Kings. We have our own team, and fans are undeniably passionate about the expansion club.

We've long known the Golden Knights would be our first major-league sports franchise, but with each passing day it gets more real. Today, obviously, was one of the noteworthy moments.

The awards show coincided with the Golden Knights expansion draft, where players such as Pittsburgh goalie Marc-Andre Fleury and Nashville's James Neal were selected to comprise Vegas' inaugural roster. Fleury, a three-time Stanley Cup champion, received a standing ovation at T-Mobile Arena, and looked surprised by the support.

It was just another example of how the Golden Knights have captured the attention of Las Vegans.

Many will tell you tonight was significant because the identity of the players was announced. And, don't get me wrong, it was pretty cool to hear majority owner Bill Foley and General Manager George McPhee list off the players one by one.

But that wasn't what stood out the most.

Rather, it was the Golden Knights fans, those diehards who are counting the moments until the season begins and showed up tonight in full force, who were most noteworthy. This is their team and they are taking ownership.

They arrived by mid-afternoon and lingered around the arena in the 110-degree heat waiting to get in. They were vocal when the selections were announced. They made it feel like Las Vegas, in fact, is a major-league city.

"There is a big buzz around the city. Everyone is looking forward to it," said Brayden McNabb, formerly of the Los Angeles Kings and one of the 30 players the Golden Knights added.

Some (I'm guilty as charged) had doubts we could pull it off. The concerns were two-fold.

First, the desert city didn't have enough hockey fans to generate a significant support system, especially for a team not expected to initially be a winner. And, secondly, many of our residents come from other cities and already have another rooting interest.

Las Vegas hockey fans packed T-Mobile Arena for the 2017 NHL Awards and Vegas Golden Knights expansion draft. (Las Vegas Sun)

While those theories aren't necessarily inaccurate, they seem increasingly irrelevant. Locals, everyone from hockey fans to people who simply love their hometown, are jazzed about the addition of the Golden Knights to our area's landscape. That was evident tonight.

"I'm looking forward to seeing our fans' reaction because they have been so dedicated. People are going to be surprised by this team," Foley said minutes before the draft.

Some of the players selected were more noteworthy than others. Some probably won't play a minute for Vegas. They'll be sent to other teams as McPhee continues to acquire entry draft picks by the masses. He wheeled and dealed for 11 draft picks during the expansion process, including two extra first-rounders on Friday.

That will give the franchise the young talent to having staying power. The staying power is what will make or break the franchise.

Residents will pack T-Mobile Arena during the initial few seasons because the team is new and everyone will want to experience a night of major-league sports. But if the team doesn't win, the fans won't come back — it's Vegas, after all, and we only support winners.

Those draft picks will form a young nucleus that can mature together and potentially transform into a winner. In the third or fourth years of the franchise, we'll start to see a team capable of competing for the playoffs. By the seventh season, when Foley has promised a Stanley Cup run, there could be that opportunity.

There also should be plenty of memorable nights against the Kings, a team that appears to be the natural rival. Each time the Kings were mentioned, the chorus of boos followed. At the very least, it's another reason to get excited.

"I will be a rival with my old team," McNabb said with a smile. ■

The Vegas Golden Knights introduce their new players and field questions from the hometown crowd following the expansion draft. (Las Vegas Sun)

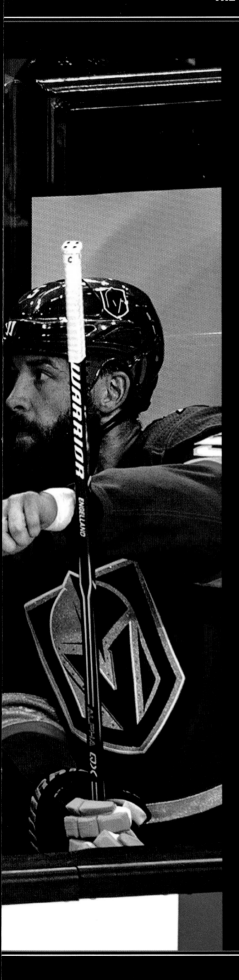

HEAD COACH

GERARD GALLANT

Head Coach Gallant Sees Bright Future for Golden Knights

By Ray Brewer | October 1, 2017

Gerard Gallant is walking through the Vegas Golden Knights' practice facility when two fans approach him.

"Hey, Turk," one calls out to him.

They ask to take a picture with the NHL expansion team's first coach. He stands between the couple, puts his arms around them and smiles for the camera.

The photo is over, but the introductions are still ongoing, and Gallant is in his element sharing hockey stories.

Like Gallant, whose uncle gave him the nickname "Turk" as a child because he would chase turkeys in the basement, the couple are from Canada. They retired here a few years ago and say they can't wait for the Golden Knights' season to begin this week.

Gallant also is eager to get started. He, too, was dealing with a hockey void after suddenly being fired in November as the Florida Panthers' coach.

In 2014-15, Gallant's first season coaching the Panthers, they won 38 games — an improvement of nine wins from the previous season. The following year, the Panthers established franchise records with 47 wins and 103 points to capture the Atlantic Division, and Gallant was picked to coach in the NHL All-Star game.

Then, last season, despite a respectable 11–10–1 record, Gallant was fired. He wasn't even allowed to ride with the team after a game in Carolina, and photos went viral online of him returning in a taxi.

"That ownership wanted to go in a different direction. I understood that," Gallant, 54, said. "Sometimes, things don't work out. That's fine. I am not mad at them. It's just disappointing because we had a good group of players. I

Gerard Gallant advises his players from the bench during a preseason home game against the Los Angeles Kings. (Las Vegas Sun)

really felt we could win the (Stanley Cup) in the next two or three years."

Five months later, the Golden Knights hired him.

"He is a great coach. He's a players' coach," said Golden Knights center Jonathan Marchessault, who played for Gallant in Florida. "He's not just a good coach but a good man off the ice, and he's a guy that makes you feel comfortable."

✦ ✦ ✦

Gallant says he learned at a young age the value of putting in work for the sport. He expects the same of his players.

When he was a child growing up in Summerside, Prince Edward Island, he spent countless hours at the local rink with friends, and would perform odd jobs there to get extra ice time. He became a top junior player — at age 16, he recorded 60 goals and 115 points in 45 games — and eventually earned a spot in the NHL with the Detroit Red Wings.

Gallant wasn't a marquee player, but he was willing to do the little things. As his 1,674 career penalty minutes in 615 games attest, he became a rugged enforcer and, therefore, a beloved teammate.

Those experiences earn him instant credibility with players, many of whom he just met a few weeks ago when the Golden Knights gathered for camp.

"I'm a guy who is 80 percent positive. I am fair," Gallant said of his expectation for players. "I expect you to work hard and compete every day to get better."

✦ ✦ ✦

Golden Knights owner Bill Foley says he wants to win a Stanley Cup within six years. Gallant won't look that far ahead.

"I don't even think about the Stanley Cup. I really don't go into a season thinking about that," he says. "I go in thinking, 'Oct. 6 — that's our first game.' Let's compete and battle, and give ourselves a chance to win that first game. Then, we'll worry about the second game and third game."

Even if the team loses this year, that could actually benefit the Golden Knights in the long term. It would help them add to their impressive bounty of draft picks — they have nine extra picks in the next three years, including six in the draft's initial three rounds.

Vegas made three first-round selections in June's draft and is stockpiling quality younger pieces for future seasons. But these players are teenagers, not yet ready for the NHL. In three years, Golden Knights officials believe they'll have one of the game's best young rosters.

But what about this season?

"We want to do what is best for our team and organization in the long term," Gallant said. "We want to be an organization that is respected, works hard, competes and battles."

This isn't a new position for Gallant. In the early 2000s, he was an assistant with Columbus when that franchise made its debut. Gallant was eventually elevated to head coach for parts of four seasons. Columbus never had a winning record while Gallant was there, and it took eight years for the team to reach the postseason.

While some will look at the struggles of Columbus, or other expansion franchises in recent memory, and assume the worst for Vegas, Gallant isn't ready to make the comparisons. He believes they are building a winning franchise with sustainability.

Like Foley, he's convinced free agents will eventually come here because of the warm winter weather and tax breaks. And the Golden Knights' facilities — the City National Arena headquarters in Summerlin and the game-day home, T-Mobile Arena on the Strip — are second to none.

As Gallant's already learned, there are plenty of great places for a photo.

"There's a real good buzz around this community with our fans," Gallant said. "We're going to give them an outstanding year." ■

Gerard Gallant speaks to the crowd after announcing the Golden Knights' expansion picks off of every NHL roster. (Las Vegas Sun)

BRIGHT BEGINNING

Thrilling Win Delivers Moment of Joy to Las Vegas After Dark Week

By Jesse Granger

As Golden Knights forward James Neal flipped the puck from his knees — over a diving goaltender and toward the net — he didn't have time to watch where it landed.

Neal crashed face-first into the end boards, but just before the collision he caught a glimpse of Stars fans through the plexiglass. Their agonized faces, halfway covered by their hands in disgust, told Neal his shot had found the back of the net.

The eventual game-winning goal in Dallas gave the Golden Knights a 2-1 victory in their first game in franchise history, but, more important, it put a collective smile on the faces of fans back home.

"I'm glad we could just give people something to be happy about," Neal said. "We went and saw the first responders and are just doing everything we can to help uplift this city and this community."

Neal attended the Route 91 Harvest Festival last Friday and planned on returning Sunday.

"I got a text Sunday night that I was skating by myself in the morning so I didn't end up going," Neal said. "Having friends there at the concert and what happened is just sickening. My prayers go out to everyone affected."

Neal missed attending the concert on the night of what would become the deadliest shooting in modern U.S. history because he was busy rehabbing his hand. The winger had surgery in July after breaking his hand in last year's Stanley Cup playoffs and only began handling a puck a week ago.

"I honestly didn't think I'd be starting the season," Neal said. "I just wanted to try to do everything I could to be a part of the first game with this team."

Neal not only scored the spectacular game-winning goal, but also the first goal in team history earlier in the third period.

"He's probably going to be pretty tired tomorrow morning, but he played well and he can capitalize on those chances and that's what a goal scorer does," coach Gerard Gallant said.

The Stars outshot Vegas 46-30, but Golden Knights goalie Marc-Andre Fleury was nearly unbeatable between the pipes.

"Fleury stole that hockey game for us," Gallant said. "He was outstanding. He made some great saves for us and he kept us in it."

Fleury finished with an impressive 45 saves, only beaten by a shot that was tipped on the way to the goal by Tyler Seguin late in the second period.

Linemates Nate Schmidt (88), James Neal (18) and Oscar Lindberg (24) celebrate the Golden Knights' game-winning goal during the third period against the Stars. (AP Photo)

"It was great to get that first game under our belt, and to win makes it even more special," Gallant said. "We played a great hockey team tonight, so we can look back and say we played one of the better teams in the league, in my opinion, and played toe-to-toe with them all night."

The turning point in the game may have come when Stars' starting goalie Ben Bishop was injured when a puck hit him in the mask. Bishop, who had saved all 12 of the shots he faced to that point, left the game bleeding from his face and was replaced by Kari Lehtonen.

Lehtonen surrendered the two goals to Neal and the Golden Knights completed the unlikely come-from-behind victory. The former Nashville Predator has 238 career goals, including one in last season's Stanley Cup Final, but says the two he scored Friday night were equally important.

"Those are up there with the best of them," Neal said. "I know it's just the first game of the year, but just seeing how happy guys were and how excited everyone was to start the season with a new team with a fresh start (was great)."

The Dallas Stars provided a moment of solidarity before the game when their players skated across the rink and stood behind the Golden Knights during the national anthem. Players know the win is relatively insignificant in the grand scheme of things happening back home.

"It's not a happy ending yet because a lot of people are still suffering," Fleury said. "But for us to be out there and win the first game, I think the guys worked hard all game to get that win. Hopefully that makes all of the people in Las Vegas proud of us."

There isn't a city at the moment that needed something to celebrate more than Las Vegas, and in their first-ever game the Golden Knights delivered. ∎

James Neal pulls pucks onto the ice for warmup before the Vegas Golden Knights' first game as a franchise. Neal was named an alternate captain for the team's inaugural season. (AP Photo)

✦ REGULAR SEASON ✦
October 10, 2017 • Las Vegas, Nevada
Golden Knights 5, Coyotes 2

A GOLDEN NIGHT

Vegas Stifles Arizona in First-Ever Home Game
By Case Keefer

Within a five-minute span Tuesday night, Deryk Engelland was a catalyst behind the crowd tearing up with emotion and yelling out in euphoria at T-Mobile Arena.

The lone longtime local on the Vegas Golden Knights' inaugural-season roster first touched the 18,191 fans in attendance with a speech to cap a pregame tribute to victims and first responders of last week's mass shooting. Then he roused them with a scorching slap shot that zipped into the net at 4:18 of the first period.

The rare score from the usual defensive enforcer was part of a four-goal Golden Knights blitz in the opening 11 minutes, which led them to a 5-2 victory over the Arizona Coyotes in their home debut.

"The guys responded after a nice little ceremony and came out flying," Engelland said. "To just get that lead and that cushion was a big thing."

For those who had eagerly anticipated a major-league professional sports franchise coming to town for years, it was a performance well worth the wait. It only took two and a half minutes of game time before they could celebrate a goal, with Tomas Nosek receiving a perfectly placed pass from Pierre-Edouard Bellemare and rocketing the puck past Arizona goalie Antti Raanta.

Engelland's only shot of the night came less than two minutes later. And then James Neal added his fourth and fifth goals of the young season, the first one on a turnaround and the second powered in after a crease pass from Reilly Smith.

"To be honest with you, I thought the start was going to be real hard for us," Golden Knights coach Gerard Gallant said. "I didn't expect us to start like that. It was a complete reversal."

The Golden Knights have defied expectations so far this young season. Pegged to be the worst team in the league, they instead stand alongside the St. Louis Blues and Toronto Maple Leafs as the only franchises to start 3-0 so far.

They're also officially off to the best start ever by an expansion franchise, surpassing the 1967 Oakland Seals and Los Angeles Kings, which both went 2-0 but lost in their third game.

"Special night," Neal said. "It was honestly unbelievable."

Neal is now tied for second in the NHL in goals, behind only Washington's Alexander Ovechkin. His second goal also broke an 0-for-11 start to the season for the Golden Knights' power play.

They failed to score on their other two advantages, however, to now make the power play a still-troublesome 1-for-13 on the year.

Golden Knights players celebrate a goal during the their first-ever home game at T-Mobile Arena in Las Vegas. (Las Vegas Sun)

"It's not a big deal to me," Gallant said. "We're a work in progress. We're working on it every day. They got a big goal tonight, and that will get them some confidence for sure."

Goalie Marc-Andre Fleury is already overflowing with confidence. He had his third straight impressive showing, totaling 31 saves.

Gallant said Vegas was gassed by the third period, and the onus to keep it afloat fell on Fleury. The Coyotes got off 18 shots on goal in the third, as opposed to only 15 combined in the first two periods, but Fleury was on point.

During one Coyotes' power play, he blocked five shots, including three rapid-fire from different directions. Arizona finally slipped one through on a hard-to-stop tipped shot from Kevin Connauton with six minutes remaining, which joined a first-period score from Tobias Rieder for its only goals.

"All of our players really believe in our goalie, and he's been A-1 for the first three games and that's what we expect of him," Gallant said. "Marc is a great character person, and we know he's a great goalie. He's going to be the leader of the team."

Fleury had a smile affixed both pre-game when he was introduced and post-game when he celebrated in the locker room. The players couldn't hide their excitement for the atmosphere at the arena.

The frills extended into the intermissions, with Cirque du Soleil's "O" performing in the first and the Golden Knights' 12-man drum line accompanied by 3D visuals overtaking the ice in the second.

The players, of course, missed those touches of the game-day experience while in the locker room. Luckily for them, the reception they received from fans was more than enough.

"It was electrifying," Engelland said. "If we can keep that crowd in it like that, it's going to be an exciting place to play." ■

Names of all the victims of the recent Las Vegas mass shooting are projected on the ice during a pregame ceremony. (AP Photo)

71
FORWARD

WILLIAM KARLSSON

Karlsson Reaching New Heights in Vegas

By Jesse Granger | November 24, 2017

Golden Knights forward William Karlsson has been so hot over the past month, it's a wonder how they keep the ice frozen beneath him at T-Mobile Arena.

"You just have to laugh at it because I've literally never seen someone as hot as he is right now," fellow Vegas forward Erik Haula said. "I just hope he continues it because it's fun to watch."

The 24-year-old Swede admits he's playing the best hockey of his life, and the numbers back it up. Karlsson scored two goals in the Golden Knights' 5-4 overtime win over San Jose Friday night, bringing his season total to 12.

It's three more than his previous career high — and it took him a quarter of the season to do it.

"I've been scoring so many goals lately, so for sure I'm playing the best hockey of my life right now," Karlsson said. "I play with two great linemates who help a lot, so I think it's a combination of everything."

Karlsson played 162 games over the last two seasons with the Columbus Blue Jackets, but scored only 15 goals combined (0.09 goals per game). Through 21 games in Vegas, he's scoring 0.57 goals per game.

"I don't know what he's doing different but he's playing a good, solid game at both ends of the ice," coach Gerard Gallant said. "That usually happens — if you play hard on one end you get rewarded on the other."

It has a lot to do with opportunity. After playing only 13:23 per game last year with Columbus, Karlsson's time on the ice with the Golden Knights has jumped to 17:52 this season.

William Karlsson had a breakout year in Vegas, racking up 43 goals and 78 points in the regular season. (AP Photo)

"That's pretty much the story of all of us," said Karlsson's linemate Jonathan Marchessault, who scored the overtime winner on Friday. "We are all guys that didn't have the chance to play on the top two lines and some didn't play at all like (Brendan) Leipsic who is playing big minutes for us. It's just fun that we can give everyone an opportunity, and I think everyone is making the most of it."

Karlsson has had his share of spectacular goals: His first of the season was a beautiful one-timer to beat the Blues in overtime. But many come because he's willing to battle in front of the net.

"I mean, everything he touches goes in," Marchessault said, laughing. "I think it's great to play with a guy like that. He's a hardworking guy and he's the identity of our group. He's not flashy but just makes the plays."

Karlsson's first goal on Friday came on a rebound following a shot by Alex Tuch. He pushed the puck to the right of the goaltender to put Vegas up 3-1 at the time.

The second came when he redirected a shot from Marchessault past San Jose's netminder to make it 4-1.

"I just positioned myself there in front of the net and it was a perfect shot from Marchessault, so I just had to tip it in," Karlsson said. "I've had some puck luck for sure. It seems like the puck is always there for me."

It's hard to equate it to luck when Karlsson is shooting with pin-point accuracy. His shooting percentage with the Blue Jackets was 7.7 — just below the league average of 8.9.

This season it has spiked to an otherworldly 24.5 percent, which is good enough for sixth in the NHL. Of the five above Karlsson in shooting percentage, only one (Mark Stone) has more goals.

It's highly unlikely Karlsson can keep this pace up for 82 games (he's on pace for 50 goals, which would have led the NHL last season), but the Golden Knights are enjoying it while they can.

"When you're hot, you're hot, and he's got a hot stick right now, so we want him shooting as much as he can right now," Gallant said. ∎

William Karlsson carries the puck during Game 5 of the Western Conference semifinals against the San Jose Sharks. (Las Vegas Sun)

29

GOALTENDER

MARC-ANDRE FLEURY

Flower Power Fuels Vegas

By Jesse Granger | December 23, 2017

Throughout the Golden Knights' remarkable start to their maiden season, one of the predominant reasons coaches and players give to explain the success is the team's depth, balance and lack of an individual superstar. Look out, because that last part may not be true.

Marc-Andre Fleury stopped all 26 shots by the Washington Capitals during the Golden Knights' 3-0 win Dec. 23 at T-Mobile Arena, recording his first shutout as a Golden Knight, and 45th of his career.

"He's our superstar in a way," David Perron said. "We managed to make some noise without him for a while and I think now he wants to join in the action."

Fleury is one shutout behind the Kings' Jonathan Quick and Predators' Pekka Rinne for third among active goalies, and has shown no signs of slowing down since joining the Golden Knights.

The win improves Fleury's record this season to 6-1-1 with a .938 save percentage. His only regulation loss came on Oct. 13 against the Red Wings when he suffered a concussion.

Prior to the concussion, Fleury stole road wins for the Golden Knights against the Dallas Stars and Arizona Coyotes where he saved 72-of-74 shots faced.

"If we remember we weren't even playing that good of hockey early in the season and he kept us alive in those games," Perron said. "I think he's just happy to be in the mix again. He wants to be just one of the guys. He's a

With three prior Stanley Cup championships to his name, Marc-Andre Fleury was a natural fit to serve as the cornerstone of a young franchise. (Las Vegas Sun)

leader because of the way he plays on the ice."

Now Fleury has returned to the lineup, but the team in front of him has drastically changed — at least the perception of it has.

Vegas is 23-9-2 and sits atop the Western Conference with 48 points. Since 1967 when the NHL expanded from the Original Six (creating two conferences) the teams leading their conference on Christmas have qualified for the playoffs 96-of-96 times.

"We knew what we got when we got (Fleury) in the expansion draft," Golden Knights coach Gerard Gallant said. "We know he's a first-class goaltender and he played a real solid game tonight."

Fleury has shut out the Capitals in consecutive games, dating back to last year's Stanley Cup Playoffs when he and the Penguins defeated Washington 2-0 in Game 7 of the Eastern Conference semifinals.

"I guess I've faced them a few times over the past few years, and I guess you pick up a few things here and there, but they have a lot of talent on the team and you can't predict all the time what's going to happen," Fleury said.

He stopped the last 55 shots by the Capitals.

"A lot of our game was that we couldn't get past Marc-Andre Fleury, but we had a couple looks," Capitals coach Barry Trotz said. "They really compete. They make those desperation plays, and I thought Marc-Andre Fleury was real strong when he needed to be tonight."

Even with a shutout, Fleury wasn't spectacular in net. Most of the time he was in good position and the defense limited the Capitals high-danger scoring opportunities. But Fleury shined in the other aspects of goaltending, like being a second set of eyes for his defensemen.

"It's incredibly helpful and it's something that's very undervalued is how a goaltender communicates to his defensemen," Vegas defender Nate Schmidt said. "He's the guy that can see the whole ice. We have our backs turned and we have to rely on him. It all starts with him being very vocal."

Another aspect of Fleury's game that helps the Golden Knights is his puck-handling ability behind the net. When he's on the ice he can sometimes work as a third defender, especially when the puck is dumped into the zone.

"It's huge," Golden Knights defenseman Shea Theodore said. "I think one of the biggest parts of his game that I like is the way he moves the puck. He's very mobile and that always helps as a defenseman. It gets you out of pinches sometimes when he's able to move the puck."

When Fleury goes behind the net to catch the puck, he's not simply looking to clear it out. There are times he holds on, assesses the situation and starts an offensive rush going the other way.

"The other guys who played really well for us don't handle the puck as much as he does, and he's got a lot of confidence doing that," Gallant said. "Sometimes it backfires on you, but the way he handles the puck definitely helps us break out of our zone."

As the Golden Knights head toward the second half of the season, hoping to stay in the playoff race and eventually make the postseason, Fleury is going to be key.

A hockey goalie, perhaps more than any position in sports, can carry a team to wins in the postseason despite what's happening around them. It's been proven year after year in the NHL playoffs that a hot goalie can propel a less-talented team to a deep run at the Cup.

And while the Golden Knights have proudly proclaimed their lack of a superstar as a badge of honor, Fleury may be just that.

"It goes without saying that he's a phenomenal player and he's the reason why we have a chance to win every night," Schmidt said. "He and (Malcolm) Subban have become a great tandem in our league and that's what you need. You need two goalies to play well and those guys are playing great." ■

Marc-Andre Fleury deflects a shot on goal while facing his former team, the Pittsburgh Penguins, at T-Mobile Arena. (Las Vegas Sun)

VEGAS, TAKE A BOW

Golden Knights Fans Give Team Massive Home-Ice Advantage

By Ray Brewer • January 3, 2018

No. No way. Never.

That was my reaction when a longtime local compared the energy inside T-Mobile Arena during a Vegas Golden Knights game to how bonkers fans were at the Thomas & Mack Center for the peak of UNLV basketball's dynasty in the 1980s and early '90s.

I was there for all those memorable Rebel games — wins against David Robinson and Navy, or when Georgetown came to town. Even when they were playing lowly league opponents in the old Pacific Coast Athletic Association (now the Big West) like Pacific or UC Irvine, the arena was sold out and so loud you couldn't hear the person talking next to you. Many in town were desperate for tickets or thrilled to go once a season.

It couldn't possibly be that way for hockey, I argued.

Then, during the national anthem Tuesday before Vegas' 3-0 win against Nashville, it was pretty clear my friend's observation was spot-on. As Paul Shaffer, yes that Paul Shaffer, arrived at the part "... gave proof through the night," a loud chorus of "Knights" chimed in.

That was just the beginning.

From the pregame hype video when the noise and anticipation mirrored that of UNLV's fireworks show back in the day, to the constant chorus of "Go Knights, Go" and the wild celebration after the Knights scored, it became glaringly obvious that Las Vegans love their team.

Vegas' Reilly Smith punctuated that sentiment when he declared in a post-game interview on display at the arena: "Our home record is because of the energy of this crowd." It drew a thunderous response.

And we weren't supposed to be a hockey city.

What's happening at T-Mobile Arena, no matter the opponent or day of the week, has become the story of the NHL season. The Knights are historically good for an expansion franchise, regardless of the sport. And just like Smith said, your support is a significant reason why.

Without the best home-ice advantage in the league, there isn't a 17-2-1 record in Las Vegas and hopes of a long postseason run. Vegas went from hoping to make the playoffs in three years of existence and competing for the Stanley Cup in five or six, to having the third-best betting odds in the league to win this year.

Many use the "Vegas Flu" theory to explain the Golden Knights' greatness at home, including wins against league notables Pittsburgh, Tampa, Toronto and Nashville. Sure, some visiting teams have allowed players to enjoy the Las Vegas nightlife, and they probably weren't at their best when the puck dropped — hence, the Vegas Flu.

But that theory does a disservice to the home team.

T-Mobile Arena's unrivaled pregame experience has included live swordfights, showgirls, the Drumbots and a giant knight's helmet. (Las Vegas Sun)

You don't assemble an eight-game winning streak, including victories at Los Angeles and against league-leading Tampa, and credit the success to other teams partying too hard the night before.

This team is good, which in all honesty is a surprise. While William Karlsson has been one of league's biggest surprises, the Knights don't necessarily have a superstar. Rather, it's a group of players who really like playing for each other and who are thriving in this unexpected winning season. They are having fun, and we are having fun supporting them.

They weren't built to win this year. The plan was to sell off key players in late February to accumulate more pieces for when they expected to contend in the third or fourth seasons. That still could be the plan, actually.

Or is it?

There's such momentum for this team around town — everything from standing-room-only practices in their Summerlin facility to reports of myriad children receiving Golden Knights gear for holiday gifts — that management would be crazy to break up the team. Add to it. Fight and claw to bring a championship to the city.

Remember, we love winners in Las Vegas. UNLV basketball became our passion because they won — and won in style. They ran up and down the court and scored with high-flying dunks and long-range 3-pointers.

The Knights are well on their way to surpassing that excitement. With each game, especially when the outcome is decided so dramatically like in victories against Tampa, Anaheim or Pittsburgh, more Las Vegans are fervently joining the fold.

Can you imagine how loud it will be for the playoffs? Kind of like that night when UNLV beat David Robinson and Navy. ■

From the very first home game, Vegas Golden Knights fans have done their part to provide the ultimate home-ice advantage. (Las Vegas Sun)

✦ **REGULAR SEASON** ✦

March 31, 2018 • Las Vegas, Nevada

Golden Knights 3, Sharks 2

PACIFIC POWERHOUSE

Golden Knights Beaming with Confidence as Playoffs Near

By Jesse Granger

William Karlsson's between-the-legs, shorthanded, game-winning goal that helped the Golden Knights clinch the Pacific Division brought the record-breaking crowd inside T-Mobile Arena to its feet.

The move to beat Sharks goalie Martin Jones was so spectacular, teammate Alex Tuch said the players on the bench were falling over each other in celebration.

"It was a 'holy crap, did that just happen' kind of moment," Tuch said, laughing. "Then we watched it on the replay and it was even better."

Karlsson's 42nd goal of the season broke a 2-2 tie and gave the Golden Knights the 3-2 win, making them the first team in the NHL to clinch a division title. He is now tied for third in the NHL in goals with Pittsburgh's Evgeni Malkin, and only three goals behind league-leader Alex Ovechkin.

"It's an unbelievable move, an unbelievable goal and it comes from a confident player," coach Gerard Gallant said. "I've seen the move before but not as smooth as that."

The key word is confidence. In a tie game, with the division title on the line, while killing a penalty, on a breakaway, Karlsson had the confidence in his abilities to put the puck between his skates and shoot from behind his back.

Karlsson said he decided he would go with the flashy move almost immediately when he got the breakaway. He said that he's been saving the move for a couple of years and that the last time he successfully pulled it off was in a lower league in Sweden when he was 18.

The confidence and poise Karlsson showed in that moment will serve him and his team well in the upcoming Stanley Cup playoffs.

"It was an unbelievable play and the kid is feeling it," Tuch said. "It takes a lot of confidence. It's a different kind of mentality and he's got it. He's got the confidence and he's rolling. This is what we need going into the playoffs. He's our leading scorer right now, and that's what we need out of him."

The Golden Knights have good reason to be confident entering the postseason. They still have a three-game road trip remaining, but Friday and Saturday's back-to-back wins over St. Louis and San Jose were an excellent simulation for what the playoffs will be like, and they aced the exam.

"I feel real good," Gallant said. "(The Blues and Sharks are) two desperate teams, they're good, heavy

Center William Karlsson celebrates his third-period goal against the Sharks, which allowed the Golden Knights to clinch the Pacific Division title. (AP Photo)

teams that play in the Western Conference and both of them are big, physical teams. I thought tonight after the first period we took over the game."

The Blues are one of a few teams the Golden Knights could face in the first round of the playoffs, and they would likely face the winner of San Jose and Anaheim if they advance to the second round.

"Those were tight games against good teams, and teams we might face in the playoffs," said Marc-Andre Fleury, who made 28 saves to earn his 29th win of the season. "The way the guys showed up tonight was amazing. It felt a little bit like the playoffs."

With their 50th win, and 107th point, the Golden Knights can be no lower than the second seed in the Western Conference, meaning they would have home ice advantage for at least the first two rounds.

"It's a great feeling to win our division," Gallant said. "Obviously nobody had those expectations at the first of the season. It's a great accomplishment, but we all know what the real accomplishment is going to be. It's all about the playoffs."

Gallant feels his team's playing style is built for the postseason.

"I'm not worried about the game changing for our group," he said. "I think our group is going to be great for it because when you watch good teams in the playoffs they're usually fast, quick and good transition teams, and that's what we bring."

As 2017-18 Pacific Division champions, the Golden Knights will have at least one more banner hanging in the rafters come the start of next season. Gallant and his players are still hoping for more.

"That's what's important to me," Gallant said. "A great regular season means a lot, but a great postseason means a whole lot more." ◼

Fans and players celebrate the Vegas Golden Knights' 2018 Pacific Division championship following a 3-2 victory over the San Jose Sharks. (AP Photo)

30

GOALTENDER

MALCOLM SUBBAN

After Slow NHL Start, Subban Emerges Strong in Vegas

By Jesse Granger | April 4, 2018

Malcolm Subban learned the game of hockey on the outdoor rinks of Toronto, where the winter air is cold enough to keep the ice frozen and players must navigate through clouds of their own breath. The Golden Knights' rookie goaltender has a lot of fond memories from those days, including one from when he was 9 years old, playing alongside his two brothers.

"P.K., Jordan and I were on one team, and we were just dominating," Malcolm says with a smile stretched across his face. He rarely shows much emotion in the locker room or on the ice, but he can't help laughing as he reminisces. "We were making tic-tac-toe passes and scoring every time. Eventually, everyone else on the team started leaving our team, because we wouldn't pass it to anyone but ourselves. By the end of the game, everyone was on the other team going against just us three, and we were still dominating. Then one-by-one, guys would just stop playing until there was no one left, and it was just us three at the rink by ourselves."

Anyone who happened to be on either side that day shouldn't be surprised that, 15 years later, all three brothers have become professional hockey players.

Malcolm's older brother, P.K., is considered one of the best players in the NHL, winning the James Norris Memorial Trophy — awarded to the NHL's top defenseman — in 2013. The Vancouver Canucks drafted Malcolm's younger

After limited playing time in Boston, Malcolm Subban has gained valuable NHL experience in Las Vegas as part of a reliable goaltending tandem with Marc-Andre Fleury. (Las Vegas Sun)

brother, Jordan, in 2013; he's currently on the roster for the Ontario Reign, the Los Angeles Kings' American Hockey League affiliate.

Malcolm is having a breakout year in net for the Golden Knights, with a 13-3-2 record, a .912 save percentage and a 2.60 goals-against average at press time.

Not only has he established himself as "the goaltender of the future," for Vegas, but he provides solace for Golden Knights coaches, players and fans, knowing the team has a capable backup during the playoff run. Starter Marc-André Fleury has already missed time twice this season and has a history of concussions.

With performances like his 41-save shootout win in Nashville on Dec. 8, and his 42-save overtime performance in San Jose on March 22, Subban has continued to show he's reliable when called upon. "I'm really confident [in Subban]," says Golden Knights leading-scorer Jonathan Marchessault. "He has proven that he's a really good goaltender. We are lucky we are on a team that has two quality goaltenders, and whoever is in net, we feel confident that we can win the game."

Subban has been injured twice himself this season, but displayed no signs of rust when he was called into action midway through a March 20 game after Fleury left with an undisclosed injury. "As a backup, that's your job to make sure that you're ready at all times," Subban says. "You want to keep getting better, especially as a young guy that hasn't played that many games. It's been great learning from (Fleury). I've learned a lot from him this year."

But the road to this moment hasn't been easy. The 24-year-old didn't start playing goalie until he turned 12. Before that, he was an excellent defenseman for his age. His father, Karl, who emigrated from Jamaica to Ontario in the

1970s, coached the Subbans growing up, and initially tried to dissuade Malcolm from playing goalie — with no success.

"I wanted to make the huge saves," Malcolm says. "My dad wasn't too happy when I wanted to switch, but he finally let me switch, and now I'm in the NHL."

Subban led the Ontario Hockey League in save percentage and goals-against average as a 19-year-old. NHL's Central Scouting ranked him the top goalie in North America before the Boston Bruins drafted him in the first round of the 2012 NHL Entry Draft.

"Obviously, I didn't know I if I would make it this far, but I love playing the position," Malcolm says. "When you're passionate about something and have the work ethic, it can take you places."

What Malcolm lacked in experience at the position, he made up for in athleticism. But he failed to live up to the sky-high expectations in Boston. In his first NHL start, Malcolm surrendered three goals on just six shots. He was benched and didn't see the NHL ice again for more than a year.

In his second start, he again gave up three quick goals and got pulled. The Bruins dropped him last summer, allowing the Golden Knights to claim him off waivers. Vegas goalie coach Dave Prior said he handpicked Malcolm — a move that has been highly beneficial for the Knights this season. Malcolm won seven straight games while Fleury missed time with a concussion.

"Sometimes, you just need a change," Malcolm says. "I didn't play as well as I wanted to in the first two games (in Boston), and it kind of stuck with me. Who knows how it would have gone, but I'm happy where I am right now."

Malcolm credits Prior with fixing his game. "I think I've gotten myself under control, and I'm not sliding

Malcolm Subban warms up at PPG Paints Arena before a game against the Pittsburgh Penguins on February 6. (AP Photo)

around and getting out of position. He's been preaching that stuff to me, and it's definitely helped my game a lot."

Subban's performance has improved drastically under Prior, winning 77.8 percent of his starts — tops in the NHL for goalies with at least 15 appearances.

For his part, P.K. has enjoyed his brother's success from afar. "It's fantastic," he says. "He's worked really hard to get there, so he's earned it."

The four-year age difference between P.K. and Malcolm prevented them from playing against each other much growing up; P.K. was drafted by the time Malcolm was 14. Their first time facing off in the NHL, Malcolm bested P.K.'s Nashville Predators in a 4-3 shootout win Dec. 8.

"When he switched to goaltender, you could see that he really had a passion for it," P.K. says. "I'm not surprised (by) where he is now."

Karl Subban attended the game and got to pose for photos with two of his sons on the ice beforehand. "It was a great moment for us, and I look forward to the moment when all three (brothers) are playing in the same game," P.K. says.

P.K. might not be surprised by Malcolm's newfound success, but that puts him in the minority. His brother has gone from perceived first-round bust to likely heir apparent to Fleury in a matter of months.

Looks like Malcolm made the right choice when he insisted on playing goalie. ■

Malcolm Subban (30) blocks a shot by Vancouver Canucks left wing Brendan Leipsic during a regular season game in Las Vegas. (Las Vegas Sun)

5

DEFENSEMAN

DERYK ENGELLAND

Engelland Embraces Leadership Role on Team and in Community

By Jesse Granger | April 25, 2018

Deryk Engelland was the leader of the Golden Knights before the team played a meaningful game in Las Vegas.

His speech prior to the Oct. 10 home opener — just nine days after the mass-shooting on The Strip — will go down as one of the most memorable moments in franchise history.

"Like all of you, I'm proud to call Las Vegas home," Engelland said in front of an emotional sell-out crowd at T-Mobile Arena. "I met my wife here. Our kids were born here. I know how special this city is. To all the brave first responders that have worked tirelessly and courageously through this whole tragedy, we thank you.

"To the families and friends of the victims, we'll do everything we can to help you and our city heal. We are Vegas Strong."

Engelland has personified leadership from the moment his name was called during June's expansion draft. Tuesday, he was named one of three finalists for the Mark Messier NHL Leadership Award, which is presented "to the player who exemplifies great leadership qualities to his team, on and off the ice, during the regular season and who plays a leading role in his community growing the game of hockey."

"It's a huge honor," Engelland said. "Especially with all of the other leaders around the league on every team. I'm just honored to be part of that group."

Newly selected as part of the Vegas Golden Knights' expansion draft, Deryk Engelland answers a question from the crowd at the 2017 NHL Awards. (Las Vegas Sun)

The other two finalists for the award are Philadelphia's Wayne Simmonds and Winnipeg's Blake Wheeler. With a career-high 23 points this season, Engelland has revived his career in the city he calls home.

"When they announced that Las Vegas was getting a team I crossed my fingers hoping I'd end up here, so then to get recognized for both of these awards was a huge honor," Engelland said. "To do it here in Vegas where I call home is even more special."

Engelland has played more minutes than any season in his career — behind only Nate Schmidt — and has scored five goals. He signed a one-year extension worth $1.5 million in January to remain with the team next season.

"His offense has surprised me a lot," coach Gerard Gallant said. "I knew Deryk as a physical, hard-nosed player, and he still does that for us but he brings a lot more than that. He plays a complete game and he's really helping young (Shea) Theodore with that matchup as partners. He's helped (Theodore) a lot but his game has also been really good for us."

Engelland is also the Golden Knights' nominee for the King Clancy Memorial Trophy, which is awarded "to the player who best exemplifies leadership qualities on and off the ice and has made a noteworthy humanitarian contribution in his community."

From the sticks for kids events, to meeting with first responders and people donating at blood banks after the tragedy, to meet and greets and helping with charity, Engelland has truly embraced Las Vegas.

"We have so many good leaders in this room that not one guy or another does more or says more," Engelland said. "It's a team effort, which is the same way we play. It's 20 guys going to bat for one another every night and that's how we've been successful."

The Golden Knights' only other finalist for a postseason award is William Karlsson, who is up for the Lady Byng Memorial Trophy, which is presented to the "player adjudged to have exhibited the best type of sportsmanship and gentlemanly conduct combined with a high standard of playing ability."

Karlsson finished third in the NHL with 43 goals this season while accruing only 12 penalty minutes.

"I guess it means I've been a good guy, and that I've had a good year," an unpretentious Karlsson said, laughing.

When general manager George McPhee joined the team he said it was important to get the right people. The results on the ice, and recognition off it, say he accomplished that to this point.

"I think (McPhee) an outstanding job of that, and this proves it," Gallant said. "It's all good people, and good fun, and that's what we talk about all the time."

Vegas has built a team of leaders, and Engelland stands out above them all.

"You want to be relied upon on the ice, and then off the ice you want to show the young guys the way to go, and help them get to a level to where they can succeed as well," Engelland said. "You just put the team in front of everyone, which most guys in this room do." ■

Deryk Engelland speaks in a pregame ceremony during the Vegas Golden Knights' home opener, honoring first responders and victims of the recent mass-shooting on The Strip. (Las Vegas Sun)

✦ WESTERN CONFERENCE QUARTERFINALS, GAME 1 ✦
April 11, 2018 • Las Vegas, Nevada
Golden Knights 1, Kings 0

STARTING STRONG

Golden Knights' Game 1 Win Shows They Can Hold Up in the Playoffs
By Case Keefer

Those who spent the season saying the Golden Knights weren't built for the playoffs can trudge barefoot uphill through miles of snow back into their caves and spare everyone the hockey lectures for a while.

Vegas looked plenty ready for the elevated stakes in the first playoff game in franchise history, beating Los Angeles 1-0 at T-Mobile Arena to take a one-game lead in the teams' Western Conference quarterfinal series.

The Golden Knights won the exact type of game the naysayers said they couldn't. They prevailed in a grueling, physical battle that featured a staggering 127 hits and six total penalties.

No matter how often the Golden Knights proved themselves and how many expansion-team records they shattered throughout the season, many pointed toward the playoffs as the team's day of reckoning. The doom and gloom only intensified with Vegas struggling to win only one of its final six regular-season games in regulation, despite the fact that all of those games came after it had already locked up the Pacific Division title.

A burlier team like the Kings, they said, would render the Knights' speedier, aggressive style useless.

It's time to get out of here with that nostalgic nonsense.

Those opinions will age as well as the quotes that were projected onto the ice pregame at T-Mobile Arena about hockey not working in Las Vegas. The Golden Knights' production staff also raised their game for the playoffs, firing up the fans with a pregame package that included flashbacks to phrases like, "terrible idea," and predictions about the team failing in the desert.

The sentiments were particularly laughable in front of a record crowd of 18,479 fans that gave the Golden Knights an invaluable advantage. Much like in their home opener, it felt like the Golden Knights were destined to ride the energy to at least one early goal.

Sure enough, Shea Theodore slapped one past Kings goalie Jonathan Quick in less than four minutes for a score that would ultimately prove enough. At that point in the game, the Kings seemed more concerned about knocking the Golden Knights around than attacking offensively.

Vegas had five Corsi — a measure of every shot sent toward the opponents' goal — before the Kings had one.

It flipped in the second period, when the Kings got an early second and then third power play. They peppered Golden Knights goalie Marc-Andre Fleury with shots, but the three-time Stanley Cup champion repeatedly held up.

Everyone discounting the Golden Knights' playoff

Goaltender Marc-Andre Fleury takes to the ice at T-Mobile Arena for the Vegas Golden Knights' first playoff game. (Las Vegas Sun)

prospects must have forgotten about the Fleury luxury.

The Golden Knights didn't get beat up, either. The Kings came out with only a slight edge, 68-59, in the hits department.

The difference was, Vegas appeared to ramp up the physicality when it made sense. Conversely, Los Angeles sometimes appeared to border on a team of goons with players like Kyle Clifford attempting to bully the Golden Knights for no apparent benefit.

The cries of Vegas' size and strength shortcomings are certain to get a second wind when the Kings inevitably trip up the Golden Knights at some point in the series. These teams are too closely contested — they're now tied at 11 goals apiece in five combined games against each other this season — for a sweep.

Even if the Kings manage to win four of the next six games and end the Golden Knights' season prematurely, however, it won't be because of a dilapidated ideal on toughness. It's a revolutionary era across all sports, and time to get away from the past.

The Philadelphia Eagles just won the Super Bowl throwing the ball 43 times with a backup quarterback, not controlling the clock with their run game. The Golden State Warriors have run roughshod over the NBA without any semblance of a traditional big man patrolling the paint. The Houston Astros won the most recent World Series with a lineup of young hitters, not trusty veterans.

That's not to say the Golden Knights will win the Stanley Cup in their first try. It's just to say that their newer-age approach won't play any part in precluding them from doing so.

It got off to a pretty decent start in Game 1 against the Kings. ■

Vegas Golden Knights players celebrate defenseman Shea Theodore's game-deciding first period goal against the Los Angeles Kings. (Las Vegas Sun)

April 13, 2018 • Las Vegas, Nevada
Golden Knights 2, Kings 1 (2OT)

BATTLE ROYAL

Haula's Double Overtime Winner Lifts Golden Knights Over Kings
By Jesse Granger

The **Golden Knights' locker room** looked more like a hospital clinic during the brief overtime intermissions Friday night than a strategic meeting room. Exhausted players devoured pizza for carbohydrates and washed it down with whatever amount of Gatorade they could keep from coming back up.

Some players wrapped their chests and backs in cold wraps, while others received leg massages to soothe their cramping, dehydrated muscles.

In the end, it was worth it.

Erik Haula deked around Kings' goaltender Jonathan Quick, slid the puck between his pads and into the goal, and the record-breaking crowd erupted into perhaps the biggest party in a city known for its late-night festivities.

Haula's double-overtime winner gave Vegas a 2-1 win, ending the game after 95 minutes of torturous, grueling hockey that left both teams battered, bruised and gasping for air.

"That's one of the best feelings in sports, finishing the game in that fashion," Haula said. "It was a long game, so it's very rewarding to come out on top."

The monumental win not only gives Vegas a 2-0 lead in the series as it shifts to Los Angeles, but the fashion in which it was won — especially the effort expended by both teams — makes it even more important.

"I don't know what tonight's game will take out of both teams," Golden Knights coach Gerard Gallant said. "I don't think the pace will be quite the same as it was because guys are pretty tired and beat up from five periods of hockey tonight."

The Golden Knights had seven players with more than 30 minutes of ice time. At times it looked like they were ready to collapse onto the ice, but then they'd take a deep breath and race down the ice for another scoring chance.

Vegas outshot Los Angeles 56-30, with Quick being the only reason the Golden Knights didn't score two, three or six goals.

"He's a two-time Stanley Cup champion and he's a great goaltender," Haula said. "We know that we need traffic and we need a lot of pucks to the net. We have to make him uncomfortable and we have stressed that in the locker room."

The Golden Knights dominated play for almost the entirety of the game but only capitalized twice.

"We just kept playing the same way and that's what we've been talking about it," Haula said. "Going into

Brayden McNabb (3), Marc-Andre Fleury (29) and Deryk Engelland (5) are exhausted and exuberant following the Golden Knights' double-overtime victory in Game 2. (Las Vegas Sun)

overtime we just stressed in the locker room to keep going after them, keep getting pucks behind them, keep playing north and keep playing fast."

Eventually Quick cracked and the game was over. The entire game — all 54 saves — was for nothing.

"It's exhausting," Golden Knights forward James Neal said. "I've been on both ends so it's tough to lose them and it's great to win them. But at the same time you have to regroup and focus on the next game because they happen quick.

"It's tough no matter what to lose games, especially when they go deep into overtime," he said. "You lay everything out on the line."

And while both teams will wake up sore tomorrow, the Golden Knights muscles will have the benefit of being up 2-0.

"It was huge," Gallant said. "We took care of our home ice advantage and that was a huge win tonight. It was another great hockey team and there are too tired hockey teams for sure."

Nate Schmidt sat at his locker after the game, his equipment strewn about the floor because he was too tired to gather it together. But even as exhausted as he was, he was still in a good mood.

"I just want to thank Haula for doing what he did, so we can get out of here, get home, get some sleep and get ready for game three," he said laughing.

On the Kings' side, coach John Stevens postgame interview had the feel of a morgue.

"It's not devastating," he said. "We expended a lot of energy but it doesn't matter if you win in regulation or in quadruple overtime, it still counts as one. They won their two home games, so we have to go home and get to work."

If one of the teams will be affected more by the energy poured into this game, it is likely the Kings.

"I think we had some young legs and they didn't play as much as some of the other guys," Gallant said. "In the overtimes, you have to play everybody. Shea Theodore can skate all day long, and when those guys are moving their feet like that, it makes a big advantage for us."

The Kings spread their minutes a lot less than Vegas and had two players (Alec Martinez and Oscar Fantenberg) who played more than 40 minutes.

Los Angeles now hosts the next two games, Sunday and Tuesday night, and will likely need them both. To survive the series, the Kings will have to win four of the next five games against the Golden Knights, who have lost four out of five only twice this season in 84 games.

"We go to their building and it's going to be harder," Haula said. "They're going to be better and we know we have to be better."

Gallant's postgame press conference, which stretched to early Saturday morning, was partially held up when the microphone went out.

"Something died," he joked.

It may have been the Kings' chances to win this series. ∎

Golden Knights left wing Erik Haula celebrates scoring the game-winning goal against the Kings. (AP Photo)

ROAD WARRIORS

Golden Knights Rally in Third Period for 3-0 Series Lead

By Jesse Granger

The Golden Knights didn't just take a stranglehold on their first-round Stanley Cup playoff series with their 3-2 win over the Kings on the road, they showed maturity well beyond their years.

Vegas took every punch the Kings could throw at them Sunday night, realizing Los Angeles would come out motivated to erase a two-game series deficit in front of its home crowd at Staples Center and biding their time to pull out the win.

With their sell-out crowd behind them, the Kings took an early 1-0 lead and outhit the Golden Knights, 28-13. Goaltender Jonathan Quick seemed unbeatable through 40 minutes, stopping all 17 of Vegas' shots, and a Kings' win to tighten the series seemed inevitable.

But ...

"No one started panicking," Golden Knights forward Pierre-Edouard Bellemare said. "There are three or four guys that talk in between the periods and they were saying, 'Boys, we're fine.' Coach came in and told us, 'I hope you guys knew they were going to come hard,' and we knew that. We are in their building and we knew they'd come hard but it's tough to do 60 minutes of that."

With seconds left in the first period, Jonathan Marchessault hit Kings star defenseman Drew Doughty with an illegal high stick that sent Doughty's helmet crashing to the ice. Doughty leaned in with a toothless smile and clapped his hands in Marchessault's face and the Kings' crowd roared.

Still, the Golden Knights kept their composure.

The expansion franchise may lack the playoff pedigree and overflowing trophy case that the Kings have, but they were the team with enough awareness to let the Kings punch themselves out and wait for a moment to strike.

"When they were coming hard we kept it steady, then at one point we realized, all right, let's try to get another step, and another step," Bellemare said. "Then suddenly our game started to flow a little bit better and we started creating more turnovers."

Vegas came out in the third period and scored three straight goals to stun the Kings and the 18,000 in attendance.

Cody Eakin struck first with his first goal of the playoffs, rifling a wrist shot past Quick to tie the game 1-1. Moments later, James Neal danced around a defender and slotted the puck underneath the goalie's pads to give Vegas its first lead.

With the Kings reeling, Reilly Smith fed William Karlsson in the slot to give the Golden Knights a

After two quiet offensive periods, the Golden Knights erupted with three straight goals from Cody Eakin, James Neal and William Karlsson. (AP Photo)

comfortable 3-1 lead with 5:16 left in the game.

"It was two games to none so we knew they'd come out and bring everything they had in the first period, and they definitely did," Golden Knights coach Gerard Gallant said.

Vegas came out of it with a 3-0 lead in the series, on the verge of eliminating their Pacific Division rival and better off for the experience. From the double-overtime thriller on Friday night to a come-from-behind win in Los Angeles, the Golden Knights have proven they have what it takes to win in the playoffs.

"You need that adversity and that's one of the things we talked about in the locker room between the second and third periods is that you're going to face adversity in the playoffs," defenseman Nate Schmidt said. "There's no way to get around it. You just have to make sure that you get yourself mentally prepared." ■

Above: Los Angeles Kings left wing Adrian Kempe battles Vegas Golden Knights defenseman Jon Merrill for the puck during the second period. Opposite: Cody Eakin (21) beats goalie Jonathan Quick (32) with a wrist shot to open the Golden Knights' scoring in Game 3. (AP Photo)

SWEEP SENSATION

Fleury Shines as Golden Knights Clinch Series
By Jesse Granger

The Golden Knights beat the Kings 1-0 Tuesday night at the Staples Center to complete the 4-0 sweep in their first-round playoff series.

A block east of the arena lies a street littered with partially constructed scaffolding and construction cones, labeled with a blue street sign with white trim. It reads: Flower Street.

The road isn't named after Marc-Andre Fleury, but after the series he just had, it should be. Flower in French is Fleur — hence the nickname "Flower."

With two shutouts in four games, allowing only three total goals in 275 minutes, Fleury just completed one of the most dominant goaltending performances in NHL history. Since 1980, the Golden Knights are the sixth team to allow three or fewer goals in a playoff series.

The Golden Knights and Kings combined for only 10 goals throughout the entirety of the series, which is tied for the second-least in NHL history for a four-game series — behind only a series between the Maple Leafs and Bruins in 1935 when nine goals were scored.

It was a goaltender duel for the ages, and Fleury bested Quick by one goal in all four contests.

"We knew when we got him we got a superstar goaltender," coach Gerard Gallant said. "He has carried our team a lot. He was huge for us, and at key times. L.A. put a lot of pressure on us the last two nights and had a lot of good chances to score, and he just shut the door."

Fleury stopped all 31 shots in Tuesday night's series-clinching win, and none were bigger than a third period save on Kings captain Anze Kopitar.

Kopitar faked out Alex Tuch with a slick toe-drag deke and walked down the slot with no one to stop him but Fleury. He fired glove-side, and Fleury swung his left arm violently in the air, just catching enough of the puck to deflect it over the crossbar.

"He's unbelievable," forward Reilly Smith said. "It's the key to our success, and obviously this series he pretty much shut them out completely."

Fleury had an equally monumental stop in the Golden Knights' 3-2 win on Sunday night, sliding across his crease at the last moment to get his pad on a low shot by Tyler Toffoli.

"Those are small details but they are huge momentum changers, and he had them the entire series," forward Pierre-Edouard Bellemare said. "Our next shift was unbelievable because of that save."

Fleury stopped 127 of the 130 shots he faced in the first-round series for an astronomical save percentage of .977. Compare that to his career playoff save percentage of .910 and it could be argued that the three-time Stanley Cup

Center Cody Eakin controls the puck during the third period of Game 4. Vegas went on to win 1-0, becoming the first expansion team in NHL history to sweep its first playoff series. (AP Photo)

champion is playing the best hockey of his career.

"I feel good but it's always one game at a time," Fleury said. "I feel confident. I think we are (confident) and I am too, but you don't want to be too high or too low because it's a long ride until the end."

In his usual self-deprecating fashion, Fleury refused to take all of the credit for shutting the Kings down.

"The team was great in front of me," he said. "They helped me out a lot by not giving up too many scoring chances."

But the numbers show that Fleury, 33, is playing at a truly elite level. He set new career-highs during the regular season in save percentage (.927) and goals against average (2.24). He's already only one shutout away from his career high for an entire postseason with two.

"He's been motivated all year," forward James Neal said. "A guy who has three Stanley Cups you wouldn't think he has to prove anything, but that's the kind of competitive guy he is, and I love having him behind us. He's been our backbone and our captain all year."

If he continues his play, the Golden Knights could make a deep run in the playoffs, possibly to the very end. Vegas will likely play the Sharks, who hold a 3-0 series lead against the Ducks, in the next round.

"I think you need a combination of everything to win," Neal said. "You need great goaltending, timely goals and unsung heroes. We've had that so far so we have to continue that."

The last time Fleury led his team to a first-round sweep it was in 2009 — the year he helped the Pittsburgh Penguins earn 16 wins and he hoisted Lord Stanley's Cup for the first time in his career.

"You never go far in the playoffs if your goalie isn't your best player. That's often the case," Bellemare said. "He's been our best player almost the whole season long. We are lucky to have him and we know it."

If Fleury maintains this level of play for three more playoff series, there soon could be a Flower Street in Las Vegas. ∎

Goaltender Marc-Andre Fleury displayed lights-out form in the Golden Knights' first round playoff series, stopping 127 of 130 shots he faced. (AP Photo)

DE-FINNING WIN

Fleury Posts 33 Saves in Game 1 Blowout
By Case Keefer

From the moment the matchup was set through Game 1's pregame festivities where a shark tank projected on the T-Mobile Arena ice, "Jaws" references abounded for the Vegas Golden Knights' Western Conference semifinal series with the San Jose Sharks.

After the Golden Knights' 7-0 harpooning of the Sharks in Game 1, it's hard not to think "Finding Nemo" would have made for a more appropriate cultural touchstone. The Sharks looked like clownfish — harmless, deluged and swimming well beyond their own depth.

And, for the sellout crowd of 18,444 fans, the game felt far more like a fun-loving family affair than any type of slow-burning horror.

Vegas vanquished any version of suspense in the opening six minutes, attacking San Jose relentlessly en route to three goals. The only thing that could have provided any scare was the sound of the crowd, which somehow shrieked a bit louder with each goal in the early going.

If Cody Eakin's goal off a deflection at 4:31 of the first period brought a wind wave of sound, then Erik Haula's successful wrister 26 seconds later bordered on tsunami levels. The reaction to Jonathan Marchessault's first playoff goal at 6:02 was certainly seismic, and by the time Alex Tuch converted on a power play, San Jose was completely capsized.

Vegas goalie Marc-Andre Fleury, as has come to be expected, was an impenetrable levee. The Sharks took 33 shots on goal — several of them on power plays, including a brief 5-on-3 opportunity — and Fleury played each of them perfectly.

Fleury famously won three Stanley Cups with the Pittsburgh Penguins, but none of those teams at any point in the playoffs prevailed in five straight games. The Golden Knights have now pulled it off in their first-ever attempt.

There's no overstating how impressive they've been. Supposedly at a stylistic disadvantage against the Kings in the first round, the Golden Knights smothered them with their speed and skating anyway.

That wasn't supposed to work against the Sharks, which used a similar approach to suffocate the Ducks in a first-round sweep even more lopsided than the Golden Knights' dispatching of the Kings. San Jose outscored Anaheim by 12 goals — as opposed to Vegas' four-goal advantage over Los Angeles — and spun its opponent silly by picking off passes and getting behind the defense.

But the Sharks appeared slow next to the Golden Knights, which glided past them time and again. San Jose goalie Martin Jones gave up only four goals all series against the Ducks.

Right wing Alex Tuch celebrates his power play goal against the San Jose Sharks, one of seven goals the Vegas Golden Knights would score in Game 1. (AP Photo)

He gave up five goals in 23 minutes before getting pulled versus the Golden Knights.

The Sharks can't blame their sluggishness on the eight-day layoff between rounds — not when the Golden Knights had an extra day off. Reason dictates that San Jose will still make this a competitive series.

Almost all analytical measures had Vegas vs. San Jose somewhere close to a 50/50 proposition. The Sharks played too strongly once they solidified late in the season to sink with such little struggle.

Maybe one iconic "Jaws" quote still pertains when it comes to Game 1 — The Golden Knights, "caught a shark, not the shark," on Thursday night. A Herculean effort may still await to reel in three more wins.

But no one should doubt the Golden Knights' ability to take this as far as possible, not anymore. Not with yet another emphatic answer in the face of a daunting challenge.

There's no primordial beast that's going to overwhelm the Golden Knights. If anything, they're the primordial beast themselves, sending the rest of the NHL in search of its equivalent of a bigger boat. ∎

No stranger to deep playoff runs, Marc-Andre Fleury was in impeccable form, recording 33 saves as the Golden Knights shut out the Sharks. (AP Photo)

TOUGH CALL

Overturned Goal Flips Momentum in Favor of Sharks

By Jesse Granger

The Golden Knights thought they had won.

Jonathan Marchessault slotted a backhand shot into San Jose's goal in overtime. The players cleared the bench and celebrated as the record-breaking crowd at T-Mobile Arena rejoiced in the excitement that Vegas had taken a commanding 2-0 lead in the best-of-seven series.

Well, not so fast.

Minutes later, after the NHL reviewed the play in the Situation Room in Toronto, officials waved the goal off for goaltender interference on Marchessault to continue the game.

San Jose forward Logan Couture scored the game-winning goal in the second overtime to even the series 1-1 and swing momentum in the Sharks' favor as the series turns to San Jose.

On the goal that was eventually overturned, Marchessault skated past Sharks goalie Martin Jones, making contact with the goalie's stick just prior to scoring. However, Marchessault never entered the crease, and many — including former NHL referee Kerry Fraser — believed it was not interference.

"Can't imagine many players, present or past, (other than goalies) would agree with interference on that disallowed OT goal," tweeted Fraser, who refereed 2,165 NHL games, including 261 playoff games and 13 Stanley Cup Finals. "Skating outside the blue paint is players territory. Jones stick encroached on that space."

The officials' decision to overturn the goal drastically affected the outcome of the game, and possibly the series. In their 28-year history, the Sharks had never overcome a 2-0 deficit, but they now had home-ice advantage.

Here are thoughts on the goal and the effect it had from players and coaches:

Marchessault: "I saw (Jones) was in his crease and I was out of his crease. He moves his blocker towards me so, I think it's just a referee's decision at that point and it didn't go our way. It's a tough decision and I didn't really think anything. If it didn't go our way, I just wanted to catch my breath and get ready to go."

Coach Gerard Gallant: "They are tough calls. We've seen them all year long and they're tough calls. It went against us tonight and you move on."

James Neal: "It's not my place to say anything. It's a tough one. It's a lot of emotions. It takes the wind out of your sails a little bit, but I thought we did a good job regrouping and getting back into it."

Pierre-Edouard Bellemare: "It doesn't matter what I think at the end of the day. They called it off. There's nothing you can do about it. They made a call

Vegas Golden Knights players wait for an official review after scoring a goal in the first overtime period of Game 2. The goal was eventually overturned, and the Golden Knights suffered their very first playoff loss. (Las Vegas Sun)

and we just have to move on and accept the decision. It's pretty simple."

Nate Schmidt: "It's tough to see because they only give you the one angle from the bench. It's tough. It's one of those calls that you obviously want to go your way and when it gets turned over it sucks. It was close and that's just the way it goes sometimes.

"Once it took a little longer than usual I thought there might be a chance that they'd turn it over. Guys were on the bench saying you have to reset and get ready to go back out there. They aren't going to wait for us to feel sorry for ourselves."

San Jose coach Peter DeBoer: "I thought that was an easy one. The spirit of the rule was called. It was goaltender interference."

Whether it was the correct call or not, the game is over.

"It's frustrating for sure, but you can't feel sorry for yourself," Neal said. "It happens and you have to look ahead. I don't think dwelling on the past is going to do us any good."

The Golden Knights were outplayed throughout the contest, being outshot 47-29.

"(The team) better be ready because we didn't show up for 45 minutes tonight," Gallant said. "We didn't play our game tonight. We played a great game (Thursday night), and tonight — whether we thought it would be easy or what we thought I don't know — but we didn't play our game tonight and it cost us big time." ■

STAR TURN

Karlsson Reaches Elite Status with Overtime Winner
By Jesse Granger

Golden Knights forward William Karlsson skated in on goaltender Martin Jones, waiting for him to make the first move.

Before Jones could blink, Karlsson flicked the puck past his blocker and into the net, silencing the sellout crowd of 17,562 inside SAP Center in San Jose as the Golden Knights topped the Sharks 4-3 in overtime to take a 2-1 series lead.

The overwhelming narrative of the Golden Knights' season has painted the team as a pack of castaways who have rallied together and created something special despite their lack of a superstar player.

Whether that narrative was ever true can be argued (Marc-Andre Fleury might have something to say about that), but after Monday night's overtime winner it's definitely over because Karlsson is a superstar.

The 25-year-old Swede has continued his 43-goal breakout season into the playoffs, leading the Golden Knights in goals (4) and points (9), the most important of which came on a laser shot to give home ice advantage back to Vegas.

"Playoff hockey is where you get your notoriety," defenseman Nate Schmidt said. "It's where you become (known as) an elite level player around the league, and I think he's making a name for himself. That's for sure."

Passing the puck never crossed Karlsson's mind on the final play, and with good reason. He has displayed historically great shooting accuracy this season. Karlsson's 23.4 shooting percentage is the highest for any player with at least 40 goals since 1994.

"I was behind him when he scored that goal, and you just see that type of thing," Schmidt said. "He does it in practice, he does it in games, big situations like that and it's incredible to watch him do that. It's so cool to watch him play and watch him become the guy and the player that he has."

Karlsson's spectacular season has often been dismissed as a fluke, but it's time to stop.

He scored two more goals than Connor McDavid, eight more than Anze Kopitar, nine more than Auston Matthews and 14 more than Sidney Crosby. His plus/minus of plus-49 was 15 points higher than any non-Golden Knight in the entire league and the fifth highest since 1999.

What will it take for Karlsson to prove that he belongs with the other names on that list?

"He scored 43 goals — what else do you want?" Karlsson's linemate Jonathan Marchessault said. "And he shows up in the playoffs, gets big goals and he's a big-time player."

Golden Knights players celebrate William Karlsson's overtime goal against the Sharks. Karlsson's heroics from the regular season have only continued into the playoffs. (AP Photo)

In the first round of the playoffs, Karlsson was almost exclusively matched up with Kings captain Kopitar and outplayed him en route to a four-game sweep by Vegas.

"There's a lot more to Karlsson than just scoring," Marchessault said. "Defensively, he's awesome and I think we have a mentality as a line to play well defensively first and goals will happen. That's what happened tonight."

Karlsson's defense has been great all season, and his passing has improved drastically as the year went on.

Monday night he assisted on Reilly Smith's goal in the second period with a tip pass so perfect it was hard to believe he did it intentionally. Karlsson received the puck just in front of the crease and deflected it behind his back to Smith, who slotted it into the wide-open net.

"It's more instinct, I'd say," Karlsson said. "I saw Reilly in the corner of my eye and I knew he was back there, so I just kind of tried to get him the puck. We have the chemistry. We think the same. We are pretty fast, all three of us, and we aren't afraid to make mistakes."

Karlsson's confidence has grown all season, crescendoing in his division-clinching breakaway goal on March 31 that he slipped between his own legs and fired into the goal. That goal was also against San Jose, and he has tormented them all season with seven goals and six assists in seven games this season.

"He's done it all year for us, and that was a huge goal tonight, obviously," coach Gerard Gallant said. "I don't know if there are any superstars on our team, but there are a lot of really good hockey players. I'm sure a lot of coaches around the league say there are some star players on this team."

Gallant is being modest, but he's wrong this time. The underdog narrative has served the Golden Knights well as motivation this season, but it's no longer true.

Karlsson is a star. ◼

Marc-Andre Fleury (29) and defenseman Nate Schmidt (88) join forces to obstruct San Jose's Mikkel Boedker. (AP Photo)

BACK TO SQUARE ONE

Sharks Tie Series With Shutout Win
By Jesse Granger

When the Golden Knights' plane touches down in Las Vegas early Thursday morning, the players will already be over Wednesday night's ugly 4-0 loss in San Jose.

The game wasn't pretty, as the Sharks dominated nearly every minute en route to a convincing win on home ice to even the best-of-seven series at 2-2. The shots on goal were an even 34-34, but San Jose had overwhelming advantages in scoring chances (19-11) and even high-danger scoring chances (11-5).

Goaltender Martin Jones made several spectacular saves and handed the Golden Knights their first postseason shutout loss in franchise history.

As forward Jonathan Marchessault left the ice for the second intermission — with his team trailing 3-0 — he swung his stick in frustration, clanging it indignantly off the goalpost.

Now he'll get a restful night of sleep in his own bed, eat a home-cooked meal and completely forget about the game.

"Midnight is a new day and tomorrow we recharge our batteries," Marchessault said. "You just start over. You can't get too high and you can't get too low. We just move on."

Professional athletes pull off unbelievable physical feats with ease — whether it's a no-look touch pass right to the tape on the stick of a player streaking down the ice at 20 mph or a blistering slapshot that finds the net with pinpoint precision.

But the mental fortitude they display may be even more impressive.

Some fans take the loss harder than the players, and most struggle to turn the page like the athletes themselves seem to do relatively easily.

"Tomorrow is a new day," defenseman Deryk Engelland said. "We get up, regroup and get back at it. I go to sleep once I get home, get up and get ready to go."

It will be a long flight home. Well, as long as a 500-mile flight on a chartered private jet can be.

"The freshest thing that's in your mind is tonight, and you're never happy when you lose," goaltender Marc-Andre Fleury said, after giving up the most goals he has in a regulation playoff game this season. "We had a chance to hurt them tonight with a win and we didn't. It's back to square one with a tied series and we just have to get ready for the next one."

The team has about 45 hours between the end of the 4-0 drubbing and Game 5 in Las Vegas to get over it.

"You can't take it with you," coach Gerard Gallant said. "We turn the page. The game is over, there's nothing we can do now. We have to get better so we'll watch some tape, talk to a few players and say we have to be better in some areas."

Luckily for the Golden Knights, their next game is

San Jose Sharks center Tomas Hertl (48) scores past Marc-Andre Fleury during Game 4. (AP Photo)

at T-Mobile Arena, where they'll be welcomed home by 18,000-plus screaming fans.

"We know the support we get at home and our players will be ready," Gallant said. "We weren't at our best tonight but we'll be ready Friday night. We knew it was going to be a great series."

The series has become a best-of-three, with two of the games being played in Las Vegas.

"We worked all year for that home-ice advantage," Marchessault said. "I think that if we battle hard and play well at home we'll be fine."

The Golden Knights have outscored opponents 13-5 at home this postseason, including a 7-0 win over the Sharks in the first game of the series.

"I'm not worried about our team," Fleury said.

Gallant is equally confident entering Game 5, closing the press conference Wednesday night with, "There's no doubt we'll be ready to go." ■

RISING TO THE OCCASION

Clutch Performance Puts Golden Knights One Win from Conference Finals

By Jesse Granger

The bigger the moment is, the better the Golden Knights seem to play.

It's been that way consistently through their inaugural season, and it continued as they beat the Sharks 5-3 to push them to the brink of elimination and move within one game of the Western Conference Finals.

Vegas raced out to a 4-0 lead before holding off a late comeback. Throughout the first 50 minutes of the game, the Golden Knights were dominant in the biggest moment of their brief franchise history.

Starting with their first game on Oct. 6 in Dallas, you can argue Vegas has won every pivotal game in its path.

The Golden Knights steamrolled the Coyotes 5-2 in the emotional home opener on Oct. 10 and blasted Winnipeg 5-2 on Nov. 10 to stop the bleeding following a rough road trip and the loss of their top three goaltenders.

They edged the two-time defending Stanley Cup Champion Pittsburgh Penguins 2-1 in Marc-Andre Fleury's sentimental first game against his former team on Dec. 14 then took down the league-leading Tampa Bay Lightning five days later.

Vegas swept the eventual Presidents Trophy-winning Nashville Predators and ended any thought of the Sharks catching them for the Pacific Division title

with an emphatic victory on March 31 to close out the regular season home schedule.

Many doubted the Golden Knights' playing style would translate to the postseason, especially against an experienced, veteran team in the Los Angeles Kings, but they promptly swept them in four games.

Friday's Game 5 was yet another echelon of pressure for the young franchise, and they handled it with ease.

"Honestly, I think we're just really confident in each other," forward Alex Tuch said. "We push each other to be our best and tonight we needed everyone's best."

The rookie scored two goals for the Golden Knights — his third and fourth of the playoffs — to assist them to a 4-0 lead early in the third period.

Vegas was fresh off its worst performance of the postseason: A 4-0 shutout loss in Game 4 where the Sharks dominated and appeared to be gaining control of the best-of-seven series.

"(The Sharks) played a great game last game, and we wanted to show them that we can do it, too," said forward David Perron, who had two assists Friday night. "I think we turn the page pretty well. We've done that all year no matter what happens."

Not only was Wednesday night's 4-0 loss the first time Vegas had been shut out in the postseason, it was its

James Neal (18), Erik Haula (56) and David Perron (57) celebrate Neal's first period goal. Haula, Alex Tuch and Jonathan Marchessault also contributed goals in the Golden Knights' 5-3 win. (Las Vegas Sun)

first loss in regulation.

"We all take it really personally when we lose a game," Tuch said. "Honestly, I think we're just really confident in each other. We push each other to be our best and tonight we needed everyone's best."

A loss would have been catastrophic for the Golden Knights, as the Sharks would have taken a two-game winning streak back to San Jose with a chance to close out the series at home.

But like they have all year, the Golden Knights rose to the occasion.

"I just think we want to win," James Neal said. "We worked all year for home ice advantage and it pays off. That's why you work all year, to have this advantage. To come back home and feel comfortable and we used it."

Neal scored the opening goal of the game with only three seconds left in the first period. Vegas outshot San Jose 15-7 in the opening frame but looked like it would enter the locker room empty-handed before Neal put a rebound past Sharks goalie Martin Jones.

Neal has experienced deep playoff runs, making it to the Stanley Cup Final last year with the Nashville Predators.

"I think you learn from different things that go on throughout a series like highs and lows," he said. "You learn about your mindset going into games and the momentum shifts from game to game. You learn a lot about yourself, a lot about your team and we are learning as we go. We keep getting better and I like that."

Game 6 in San Jose is an opportunity to end the Sharks' season.

"We have to know what we're going up against," Neal said. "Their backs are against the wall, so they're going to be do or die. When a team is like that, they're going to play their best hockey, so we have to recognize that and play our best. It's the toughest game."

The Golden Knights have given no reason to believe they won't be up for it.

"It's a confident group," coach Gerard Gallant said. "We're not a cocky group or an overconfident group. We just come to work, do the best we can and hopefully that's good enough to win." ■

Golden Knights center William Karlsson (71) battles to keep the puck away from San Jose Sharks center Melker Karlsson (68) during Game 5. (Las Vegas Sun)

GOLDEN DEPTH

Unsung Heroes Emerge in Series-Clinching Win
By Jesse Granger

Every day when the Golden Knights finish practice — long after the star players have changed back into their street clothes and the hundreds of crazed fans have filed out of City National Arena — the sound of pucks crashing against the glass and skates cutting through the ice lingers.

It's the sound of players trying to earn their way into the lineup.

The healthy scratches (players not part of the active 20-man roster on game days) remain after practice to work, improve and stay ready all season for the Golden Knights. Now, deep in the playoffs, the team is reaping the rewards.

The Stanley Cup playoffs are often described as a prolonged, torturous stretch of hockey that leaves teams mangled. The roster that emerges from the heap the healthiest often wins.

But the Golden Knights are now halfway to hoisting the Cup and have more players than they can use. The Knights on Sunday advanced to the Western Conference finals by eliminating the Sharks in six games.

"It shows the depth of our team," forward Pierre-Edouard Bellemare said. "We have three guys that have come into the lineup in the last two games and it's not easy to do that. Those guys have been waiting and preparing, and they have done an unbelievable job."

Oscar Lindberg, Luca Sbisa and Ryan Reaves hadn't played a minute in the postseason until the last two games against the Sharks. Reaves' number was called due to an injury to fourth-line forward William Carrier; Sbisa and Lindberg were inserted by coach Gerard Gallant to provide a spark.

"Hungry guys ready to play," Gallant said after Friday's win. "I want competitive guys in there playing. When you lose a game sometimes you go through with your coaching staff and see a guy like Lindberg working hard in practice."

Vegas has played 15 forwards and seven defensemen in the postseason.

"It shows how much character we have in the room and how much guys are ready to just jump in and play for the team," Bellemare said. "It's not fun to lose guys, but it's cool to see the guys that come up late like this bring new energy and not even look like they missed any games."

Reaves made his playoff debut in Sunday's win, leading the team with eight hits in 10 minutes of ice time after sitting out the previous nine games as a healthy scratch.

"You just stay ready," Reaves said. "You work during practice and after practice to make sure you're ready

Deryk Engelland (5) checks Sharks center Tomas Hertl (48) in front of the net during Game 6 in San Jose. (AP Photo)

BACK AT THE GOLDEN KNIGHTS' HEADQUARTERS...

for the game pace. I was keeping it simple but playing hungry still. In playoff hockey everything gets ramped up, so I definitely didn't want to pick up where I left off, that's for sure."

The players' willingness to sit out and still work hard is equally impressive. Every player says the right things when they're benched, but these Golden Knights seem genuine.

"Obviously you never want to be taken out of the lineup, but I don't think I was playing my best hockey for the last three weeks of the season and you have to go with the best lineup," Reaves said.

Having too many quality players can only be a good thing, unless they don't react well to sitting out games.

"Our guys trust each other, and that's something you can't build over time," defenseman Nate Schmidt said. "That's something that you need to know in the locker room with what you have, and I believe we have it with this group."

After losing to the Golden Knights in six games, Sharks coach Peter DeBoer wasn't most impressed by Vegas' relentless forecheck, its 43-goal scorer in William Karlsson, or its all-star goalie Marc-Andre Fleury.

"I thought we were the hardest working team in

Vegas Golden Knights players celebrate their six-game victory over the San Jose Sharks to clinch a spot in the Western Conference finals. (AP Photo)

the league before this series, but this team works hard every day for Gerard (Gallant)," DeBoer said. "Vegas deserves to be moving on. They played great. They finished the chances when they needed to. I wish them the best of luck."

The Golden Knights now await the winner of Nashville and Winnipeg, who will battle it out for at least one more game while Vegas gets even more rest.

"They're both great, outstanding teams," Gallant said. "I hope they play a bunch of periods of overtime tomorrow night, and they go seven games and the same thing happens again."

Even Gallant, who seems practically incapable of making a wrong move with the lineup, gets a few days of tranquility.

"I'm going to go home tonight and relax," he said with a giant smile. "I still have my grandkids there, so the next couple of days are going to be awesome. Getting up at 6:30 and playing with them for a while." ∎

'NO EXCUSES'

Vegas Looks to Bounce Back from Game 1 Loss
By Jesse Granger

This wasn't the start the Golden Knights were looking for. After all, they rarely trailed by three goals in the initial eight minutes of a game this season.

But that was what transpired in the first period of the Western Conference finals today against host Winnipeg, which also had its way physically with Vegas in a 4-2 Game 1 victory.

The Jets' bruising big man Dustin Byfuglien scored 1:05 into the contest and led an avalanche of offense that proved too much for Vegas to overcome. He also lived up to his hard-hitting reputation by leaving rookie forward Alex Tuch with a laceration across his nose after a jarring open-ice hit in the third period.

Vegas never trailed in its previous two series to reach the conference finals. Now, they are in an unfamiliar spot — playing from behind.

But the players aren't discouraged. In fact, they can't wait to play again on Monday.

"We are going to see what kind of team we are," Vegas forward Jonathan Marchessault said. "It's definitely a must-win next game and I think as a group everybody needs to step up, not just one or two guys."

The last time Vegas came off a long layoff, following their first-round sweep of the Los Angeles Kings, they pounded the San Jose Sharks 7-0 in the first game. This time around that wasn't the case, as they ran face-first into a Jets team fresh off a momentous Game 7 win over Nashville.

"It wasn't the start we wanted. They played two days ago so they were game-ready and we weren't," Marchessault said. "It was a good push but we knew they were going to come. It's part of the game, and we faced some adversity in the first, but the second and third were better I thought."

Winnipeg scored three goals in the first eight minutes, and the Golden Knights never recovered. But there is reason to believe they will bounce back.

"I felt in the second and third we were playing more of our style," defenseman Shea Theodore said. "I thought we were playing fast, getting pucks in and harder on the forecheck."

The Golden Knights had more chances than the Jets after that initial rush to start the game — a scoring outburst largely fueled by the electric atmosphere created by the sell-out crowd that covers the stands in a white blanket.

Vegas had a 31-18 advantage in Corsi over the final two periods of the game. Corsi tracks all shot attempts, even those that go wide of the net or are blocked by a defender on the way to the net.

While the Golden Knights finished with only 21 shots on goal — which is tied for the fewest in franchise history — they created a lot more offense than that number suggests.

"There was an awful lot of offense there, that we got a stick on or they missed on," Jets coach Paul Maurice said. "They are a very, very dangerous team. They don't

Winnipeg Jets captain Blake Wheeler gets dumped over the boards by Ryan Reaves (75) during Game 1 in Winnipeg. (AP Photo)

need a lot. You look at the score when it's 4-1 and we had some exciting chances that didn't go for us, but they also had a lot in that game."

Winnipeg's forwards did an outstanding job of sacrificing their bodies, racking up 22 blocked shots. While that effort should continue throughout the series, it's likely more of those shots will get through to Connor Hellebuyck.

As the Corsi chart by Natural Stat Trick shows, Winnipeg was spectacular in the opening period, but as the game wore on, the Golden Knights got better.

"We knew their team speed is very intimidating, so we wanted to limit their time and space," Winnipeg captain Blake Wheeler said. "That was an emphasis for us and I thought we did a pretty good job."

Maurice knew the game was closer than the score

reflected, and going forward the Jets will have to improve as Vegas does.

"They are a good hockey team and they're going to get some of those, so it's a matter of trying to limit them as much as we can," he said. "I thought we did a reasonably good job of it, but we'll have to be better at it next game. In the rush they have a lot of confidence and why wouldn't they? They complete those cross-ice passes on the way up the ice and into the offensive zone."

The Golden Knights have yet to lose two games in a row this postseason, and they badly need that streak to continue.

"There are no excuses," Marchessault said. "Everybody has to be ready to play our best game of the playoffs, and we are going to show what kind of team we are." ∎

GETTING EVEN

Feisty Marchessault Wills Golden Knights to Crucial Game 2 Win

By Jesse Granger

Golden Knights forward Jonathan Marchessault didn't mince words after the Game 1 loss to the Jets on Saturday night.

A particularly feisty Marchessault stared through the bright lights and bouquet of microphones in the crowded locker room, told reporters the next game was a "must win" and that "we are going to show what kind of team we are."

Monday night Marchessault backed his words up with a magnificent performance on the ice.

He scored a pair of dazzling goals for the Golden Knights as they topped the Jets 3-1 to knot the Western Conference finals series at 1-1 heading back to Las Vegas.

"I'm definitely satisfied with our effort tonight," Marchessault said. "Every time we need a big game out of our group, we show up. I think we showed the hockey world that we earned the right to be here, and we are able to play against a great team."

Coach Gerard Gallant wasn't fond of the use of the term "must win" after the first loss, but Marchessault simply can't help himself.

The scrappy 5-foot-9 forward may be the smallest guy on the ice most of the time, but the competitive fire that burns inside him extinguishes any physical disadvantage.

"That's the reason why we love him," defenseman Nate Schmidt said. "You know what you're going to get out of him, and when you know what you're going to get out of a guy, it allows you to go out and do your job. You have to bring your A-game to get to that same level."

Linemate Reilly Smith found Marchessault midway through the first period as he was streaking through the neutral zone and fed him a pass right onto the tape of his stick. Marchessault screamed past the Jets defense for a breakaway, and effortlessly deked the goalie before sliding the puck between his pads for the goal.

"That line was incredible," Schmidt said. "We had a really good team win tonight, but some guys really elevated their game to another level."

Vegas was nursing a 2-0 lead entering the third period, but the Jets fought back. Kyle Connor snuck a shot through Marc-Andre Fleury to cut the deficit to one goal with 12:43 to play in the game.

The sold-out Bell MTS Center exploded in celebration and the Jets appeared to have swung the momentum in their favor.

Before the fans were even able to sit back down, Marchessault skated to the front of the net, received another perfect pass from Smith, and backhanded the puck

Tomas Tatar, a healthy scratch for the previous three games, opens up scoring for the Golden Knights in the first period. (AP Photo)

past Connor Hellebuyck to seal the game for Vegas.

"He's a good player; he finds those soft areas unbelievably well, and he goes to the net hard," Smith said. "He's a small target but he's always there."

Marchessault regularly gets into altercations after the whistle with players who tower over him. His competitiveness runs outside of the hockey rink as well.

"Anything that we do whether it's soccer, basketball, when we're hanging around playing cards," Schmidt said, laughing. "He's always fired up, and he's easy to fire up too, which is the best part."

Players have commented on Marchessault's inability to handle losing to teammates on the miniature basketball hoop they have at the practice facility, so getting him fired up for a crucial game in the Western Conference Finals isn't difficult.

"If you're going to go out there and talk to the media, and say the team has to be better, then you need to lead by example," Marchessault said. "I tried to do that tonight."

Marchessault leads Vegas this postseason in goals (6) and points (15).

"It was definitely an important game for our group," he said. "Our effort last game was good but not good enough. I wanted to step up and do my job the best, and I'm satisfied with my game."

The win drastically changes the dynamic of the series. A Jets win to take a 2-0 series lead would have given them about a 90 percent chance to win, but Vegas has now tied things up, with the majority of the games remaining at the friendly confines of T-Mobile Arena.

"You're playing against great players and that's what you want," Schmidt said. "You want to test yourself every night and you want to be able to leave your mark on the game. We have to make sure we come out with the same intensity that we did tonight and maybe a little bit extra.

They aren't going to roll over for us, they're going to come back with a great game."

The chip lodged on Marchessault's shoulder appears to be permanent. The 27-year-old led the Florida Panthers with 30 goals last season (seven more than the next-highest scorer), yet the team exposed him during June's expansion draft.

This year in Las Vegas he proved his breakout season was no fluke, with 27 goals and 48 assists, and is now leading the Golden Knights in the playoffs.

"That's the story of our club," Marchessault said. "We were all (considered to be) not part of the center of our (former) teams, and everybody seized the opportunity here, and that's what has made our success."

Marchessault may be more brash about it, but his demeanor represents the overall feel of the team and plays a considerable role in their success.

"We are just a bunch of hockey players who wanted to find a home and we did," he said, "and we've been awesome." ∎

The Vegas Golden Knights bounced back from their Game 1 loss to the Winnipeg Jets with goals from Jonathan Marchessault and Tomas Tatar, plus 30 saves from Marc-Andre Fleury. (AP Photo)

JET LAG

Marchessault Maintains Postseason Hot Streak Against Jets
By Case Keefer

f Jonathan Marchessault would have driven his customized Golden Knights Lamborghini to Game 3 of the Western Conference Finals in the same manner he skated, he may have been arrested and unavailable to play.

Luckily, the Golden Knights' postseason points leader saved the speeding for the ice. He topped out within 30 seconds of the first home game of the series against the Winnipeg Jets.

Marchessault took off, the "81" on the back of his jersey blurring, as soon as Brayden McNabb poked the puck away from the Jets during their first trip into the offensive zone. Jacob Trouba, the Jets' top defenseman, had a head start but moved like a semi-truck next to Marchessault, who corralled the loose puck and spun goalie Connor Hellebuyck silly with his second straight backhanded goal of the series.

Marchessault's third overall goal of the last two games and seventh of the playoffs set the tone for Vegas' 4-2 victory over Winnipeg Wednesday night to take a 2-1 series lead.

He also put the finishing touches on the win with three seconds remaining by scoring on an empty net.

The final goal gave him his 92nd point of the overall season, surpassing William Karlsson's 90-point total for the team-high. Marchessault belongs at the top of this team; he represents so much of what's great about the Golden Knights.

The team's production staff treated the announced attendance of 18,477 fans to another adrenaline-pumping pregame package full of soundbites about how a team of outcasts in the desert could never make an impact in its inaugural season. Marchessault almost certainly heard some of it — not that he needed to.

One gets the sense that, like so many great athletes before him, all the slights are ever on his mind — headlined by the Florida Panthers leaving him unprotected in last June's expansion draft. At a time when coach Gerard Gallant and other players downplay the season-long bond from being a team of castoffs, Marchessault is still openly embracing it.

After his assertive Game 2 performance, he noted how none of the Golden Knights were considered to be "the center of our (old) teams." It's easy to see how Marchessault has internalized perceived shortcomings in his own career.

Reportedly not protected by the Panthers in part because of a concerning plus/minus — he was minus-21 for the season last year — Marchessault responded by ranking second in the NHL in the regular season behind

The Golden Knights celebrate Jonathan Marchessault's third-period goal, which sealed Vegas' 4-2 win. (Las Vegas Sun)

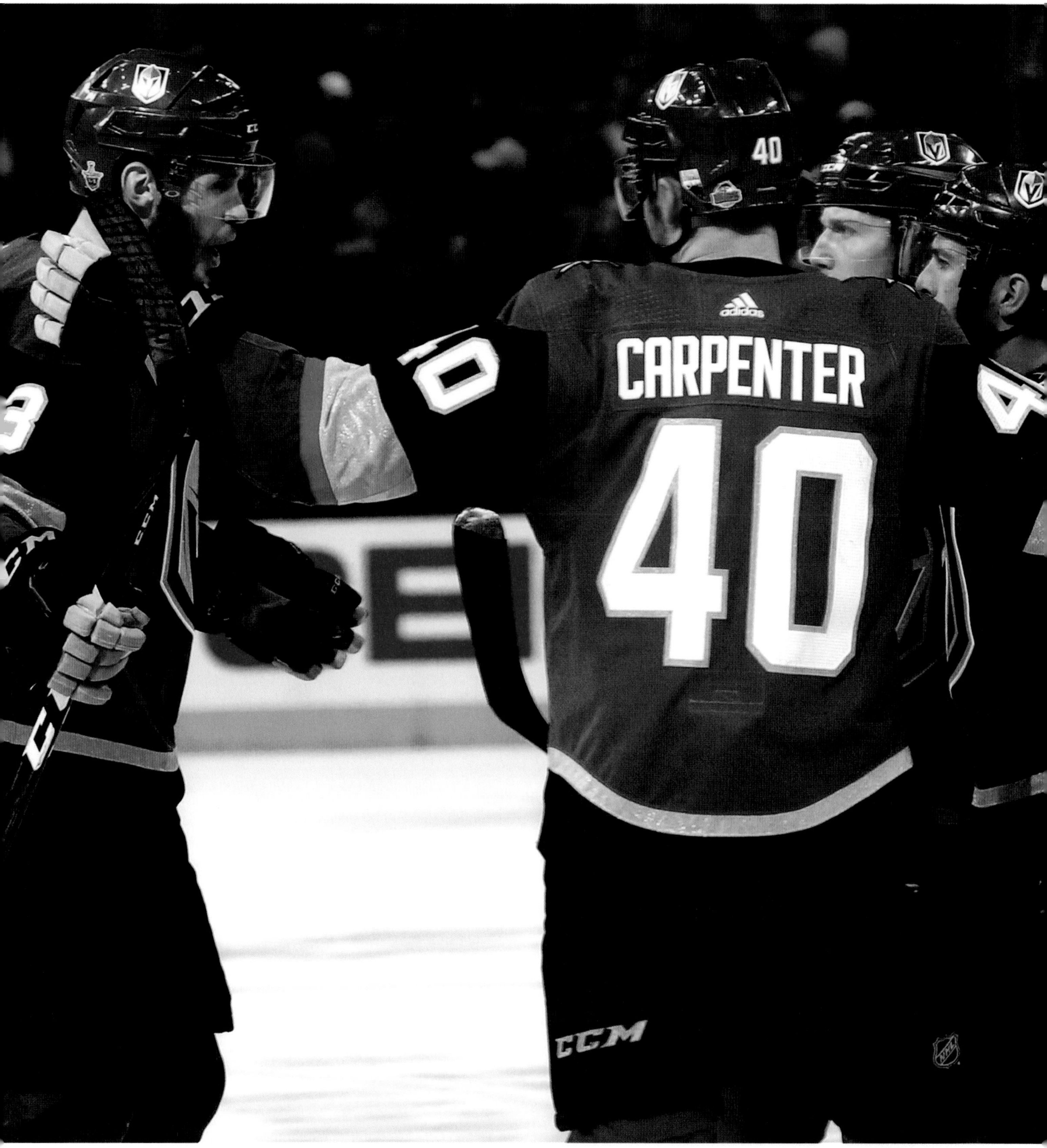
CARPENTER
40
CCM

Karlsson with a plus-36. He's also now tied for the playoff lead with Washington's Brooks Orpik at plus-12.

And the best part? He'll never draw the ire of Kendrick Lamar and fake humble because someone else is insecure.

"He's a cocky little guy," Gallant said with a smirk earlier in the day. "He jumps around in the locker room, he has a lot of fun. He has lots to say. Our players love Marchy. Some people might take him the wrong way, but I know in our locker room, our group, they really like him a lot."

So much, it seems, that they often take on the 5-foot-9 fireball's personality. Maybe it's a partial Napoleon complex, maybe it's a simple desire to prove everyone wrong.

Whatever it is, the Golden Knights do it well.

Two of the Jets' most commonly cited advantages coming into Game 3 were their power play and defense. The Golden Knights might have put together their best penalty kill of the postseason in the first period with the Jets finding virtually no scoring chances, and their only other one of the game went almost as smoothly.

Marc-Andre Fleury was as sharp as ever in net with 33 saves, but he didn't have to do much for the first half of the game. The Golden Knights' defense was relentless, particularly in the first period when they allowed only three shots on goal.

After this win, the whole team deserves to walk like Marchessault when he exited his Lamborghini pregame, a gait that may surpass one of Conor McGregor's strolls into the octagon for the most confident entrance in T-Mobile Arena history.

Marchessault wasn't one of the more popular Golden Knights during the season. His jersey sales seem to pale in comparison to the likes of Fleury, James Neal, Karlsson and even the injury-reserve designated Clayton Stoner — ah, the perks of a last name.

That's going to change quickly if Marchessault's tear leads the Golden Knights to two more wins and a Stanley Cup Final appearance. It should probably change either way.

With apologies to Chance the Raptor, Marchessault is the most fitting mascot of this continually extraordinary team. ■

Center Jonathan Marchessault's goal just 35 seconds into Game 3 gave the Golden Knights an early 1-0 lead. (Las Vegas Sun)

ON THE BRINK

Fleury Dazzles Again as Vegas Grabs 3-1 Series Lead

By Case Keefer

Everyone in the hockey world has paid attention to the Vegas Golden Knights as they've extended the greatest expansion season in any major sport — everyone except for Winnipeg goalie Connor Hellebuyck, apparently.

At the least, some of the particulars must have eluded Hellebuyck. You know, like the part about how the entire roster jelled so quickly because of the motivation they all shared from their former franchises leaving them unprotected in the expansion draft.

The Golden Knights have shown a transcendent ability to channel disrespect, perceived or otherwise, into fuel for their performances. So ignorance must be the easiest way to explain to Hellebuyck's comments Wednesday night when asked about Marc-Andre Fleury's routine of soon-to-be legendary saves in Game 3.

"I like my game. I like it a lot more," Hellebuyck said. "I like my details and will continue chugging away and getting better every single day."

Go ahead and put those words right next to Drew Doughty's quote guaranteeing the Kings would be better than the Golden Knights in T-Mobile Arena's pregame presentation if Vegas reaches the Stanley Cup Final. And the odds that it will reach the Stanley Cup Final are pretty strong now, after Vegas defeated Winnipeg 3-2 Friday night at T-Mobile Arena to take a decisive 3-1 lead in the Western Conference Finals.

The biggest reason why? Fleury has been a whole heck of a lot better than Hellebuyck.

The Golden Knights' skaters have held their own against the Jets' loaded four lines, but they've been outshot every game — including by a series-high nine shots on goal in Game 4. The teams' Corsi — a measure of every shot sent toward an opponents' goal — are even more lopsided, with Winnipeg plus-44 in the series.

The numbers haven't hurt Vegas because it often seems like Winnipeg has been firing into a brick wall. The Golden Knights' resistance, meanwhile, has been closer to a cardboard cutout with a few convenient holes.

Fleury had a .945 postseason save percentage through the first three games of the Western Conference Finals to Hellebuyck's .922. The gap is only going to widen after Fleury made 36 saves in Game 4 to Hellebuyck's 26 saves.

The eye test indicated the two goalies are even further apart than the statistics indicate — details and all.

It's hard to imagine Fleury in his current form letting two of the three goals Hellebuyck allowed on Friday to get through. The Golden Knights' latest opening-minutes

Jonathan Marchessault celebrates after William Karlsson's goal gave the Knights a 1-0 lead in the first period. Marchessault assisted on the goal.
(Las Vegas Sun)

score would have been tough for anyone to stop, as Jonathan Marchessault continued his hot streak with a beautifully precise pass to William Karlsson for a goal 2:25 into the game.

But Vegas' latest immediate answer to a Jets' momentum-shifting goal — this one came in 43 seconds as opposed to Game 3's 88 seconds and Game 2's 12 seconds — fell largely on Hellebuyck. He failed to control a shot from Pierre-Edouard Bellemare, who got his own rebound, wrapped around the net and found Tomas Nosek for an easy goal from Vegas' fourth line to put it back up 2-1.

Winnipeg's pair of goals both came after wearing down Vegas' defense, and by extension Fleury, with pressure, the second at 5:34 of the third period when Tyler Myers slapped one past him.

But Reilly Smith found himself on a breakaway with less than seven minutes to go, and many in the arena stood with a strong sense of what would come next. He froze Hellebuyck for the game-winning goal.

Put Fleury in Hellebuyck's spot and that's a much fairer fight.

In the game's immediate aftermath, there's no way to tell if Hellebuyck's boast got back to Fleury, but the Golden Knights locker room was aware of it. Vegas' most confident confirmed trash-talker, Marchessault, could barely believe it.

"Did he actually say that?," Marchessault queried earlier in the day before being assured they were Hellebuyck's words, and then asked which goalie he would take.

Marchessault kept his answer concise.

"Fleury, not even a question."

Hellebuyck is only 24 years old, with the majority of what will likely be a standout career ahead of him. But he's going to have chug awfully hard to compile a résumé that can rival Fleury's — which includes three Stanley Cup championships and six conference finals appearances so far.

Let's just say the Golden Knights like Fleury's game; they like it a lot. ∎

Marc-Andre Fleury made 36 saves in Game 4 against an aggressive Winnipeg Jets offense. (Las Vegas Sun)

REWRITING HISTORY

Golden Knights Aren't Concerned with Tradition — Just Winning
By Jesse Granger

When the Golden Knights clinched a berth in the Stanley Cup Final on Sunday, the players continued their path of total disregard of history, records and tradition that has led them to hockey's holy grail.

When the clock hit zero and the Golden Knights completed their 4-1 series win over the Winnipeg Jets to advance to the final, the players climbed over the bench and raced to celebrate with their leader, Marc-Andre Fleury.

Most congregated in one giant huddle while some like Jonathan Marchessault and Erik Haula embraced individually while leaping off the ice in pure euphoria.

NHL officials rolled a carpet onto the ice and placed the Clarence S. Campbell Bowl — awarded to the conference champion — on a round table cloaked in a black tablecloth.

Without a moment's hesitation, Deryk Engelland skated up to it, posed for a picture and lifted the trophy off the table. He carried it in celebration through the tunnel and back into the locker room.

Nearly all of the sold-out crowd at Bell MTS Place stayed after the final buzzer to cheer their Jets on one last time despite the disappointing end to their season.

When Engelland touched the trophy, a collective gasp echoed throughout the arena.

Many NHL players — and fans, apparently — think it's bad luck to touch the conference championship trophy, and doing so is a bad omen with a series still to be won to hoist the trophy they really want: Lord Stanley.

But if there's one thing the Golden Knights have shown during this unbelievable maiden campaign, it's that they do not care about tradition. They've done nearly everything contrary to popular belief, from their in-game entertainment that includes showgirls and the Blue Man Group dancing in the stands, to their up-tempo style of play that many believed wouldn't translate to the playoffs.

"We talked about (touching the trophy) beforehand as a team," Jonathan Marchessault said. "We went against the odds all year."

Why stop now?

The Golden Knights have done things their way to get to this point. A place that four franchises have never seen.

The Blue Jackets, Wild, Coyotes and Jets have been in the NHL a combined 60 seasons and have never made the Stanley Cup Final. The Toronto Maple Leafs haven't been to a Stanley Cup Final in 51 years. The Golden

Alex Tuch celebrates his first-period goal against the Jets. Ryan Reaves, acquired by the Golden Knights at the trade deadline, added the decisive goal in the 2-1 victory. (AP Photo)

Knights just made it and 544 days ago they didn't have a team name.

"We are going to keep doing what we do best and that's proving people wrong," Marchessault said. "Whoever we're facing we probably aren't going to be favored next round, so that's just the way it goes."

He's half right. According to Jeff Sherman, manager of the Westgate Las Vegas Superbook, the Golden Knights will open as plus-130 underdogs if they face the Tampa Bay Lightning in the final but minus-140 favorites if they play the Washington Capitals. Tampa Bay leads the series 3-2.

"All of the work that we've done, if we come up short it will mean nothing," Marchessault said. "Obviously all of those records and everything doesn't mean anything if you aren't the last team standing, and I think we have a lot of gas left."

The records Marchessault speaks of are too numerous to list and include his 18 points as the most during a postseason for a team in its first playoff run. The team has rewritten the record books all season and doesn't appear ready to stop.

"It gives you chills, honestly," Erik Haula said. "You just try to enjoy the moment because this is what you dream of and you can only hope for a chance to play for the Cup and that's what we have right now."

That's why grabbing the trophy is the right thing to do. Ask the 1996 Florida Panthers — who won the Eastern Conference, lost in the final and haven't been back since — if they would enjoy that moment if they could go back in time.

Not every Golden Knights player was eager to grab the silver bowl. This is, admittedly, a deep-rooted superstition.

"I wasn't going to touch it," Alex Tuch said, laughing. "I'm a rookie so I follow what they say. If they tell me to touch it, I'll touch it, if they tell me not to, I won't. Notice

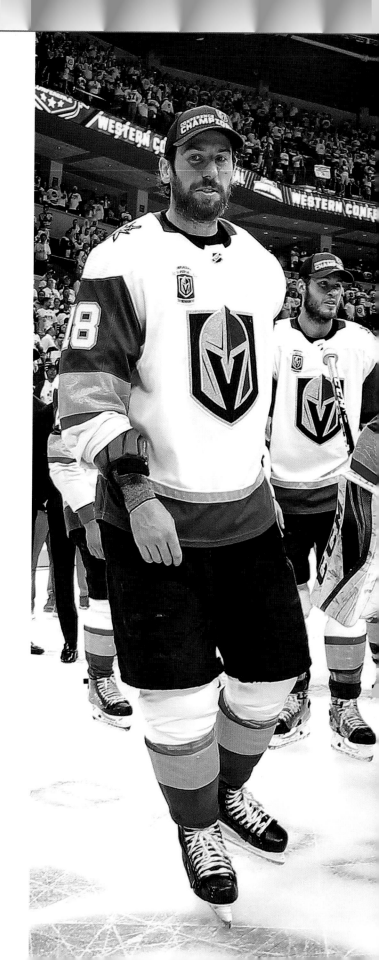

James Neal (18), Deryk Engelland (5), goaltender Marc-Andre Fleury (29) and the rest of the team show off the Clarence S. Campbell Bowl, awarded each year to the Western Conference champions. (AP Photo)

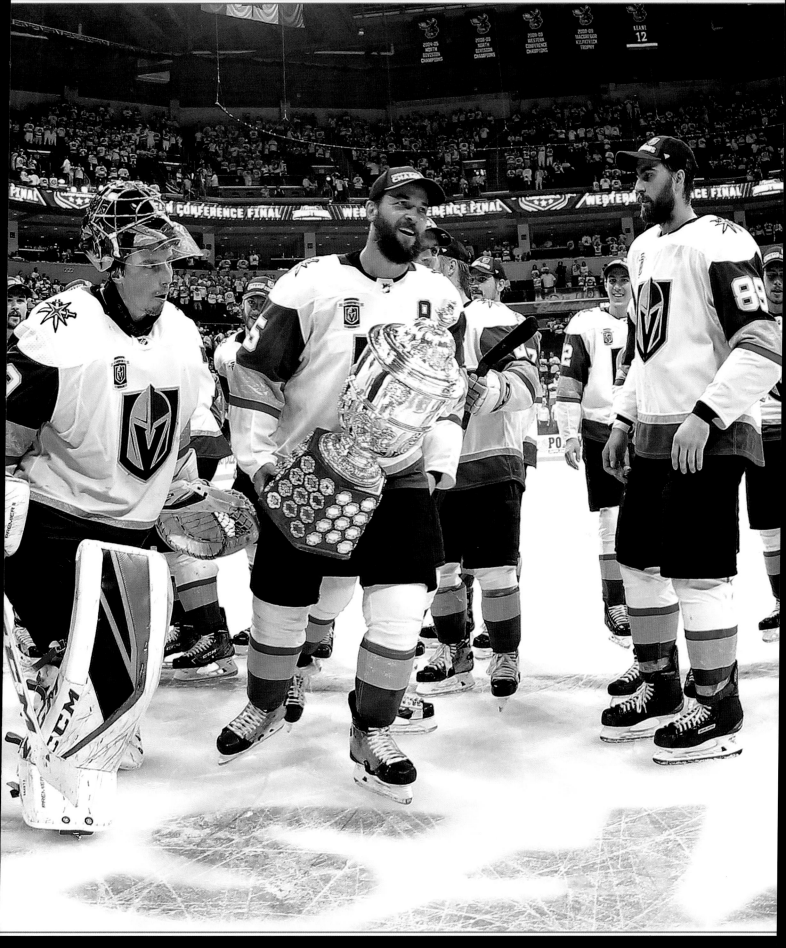

I haven't trimmed the beard or the hair at all. I'm not touching anything. I'm all in and our whole team is all in."

Nate Schmidt felt his share of playoff heartbreak in his time with the Capitals and wasn't going to be the first one to lay a finger on the trophy.

"I don't have superstitions and I really don't see anything behind it, to be honest," Schmidt said. "It was probably Engelland's decision and I'm not going to say anything to him. He's a lot bigger than I am so I don't really disagree with a lot of things he says or does. He can do things with his fists that I can't, so he can do whatever he wants."

But while Engelland had the honors of lifting it first, it wasn't his decision at all.

"We went with the experience here," he said during the postgame press conference, putting his hand on the shoulder of his three-time Stanley Cup champion goalie. "(Fleury) has been the backbone for our team. It more or less came down to whatever he wanted to do."

Fleury went to four Stanley Cup Finals in Pittsburgh. He went 3-0 in the final after his team touched the conference championship trophy and lost the time they didn't.

When Engelland caught the Canadian crowd off guard by nonchalantly grabbing the trophy, it certainly wasn't the first time the Golden Knights shocked the hockey traditionalists, and it likely won't be the last.

"We are a group of guys that didn't find a home last year," Marchessault said, referring to players being exposed by their former teams in the expansion draft. "We are all in the same situation and we want to battle for each other. I think everybody out here is a great teammate. When someone gets a goal we are all happy for them. There's no jealousy, no competition, just happiness for everyone and it's a big family." ∎

Brayden McNabb (3) and Marc-Andre Fleury (29) defend the crease from center Mathieu Perreault (85). (AP Photo)

KNIGHTS TO REMEMBER

Fourth Line Thrives Late in Stanley Cup Final Opener

By Jesse Granger

In Vegas, this is how we do the Stanley Cup Finals.

Rapper Lil Jon performed a concert for thousands of fans outside T-Mobile Arena before the Vegas Golden Knights took on the Washington Capitals, soul singer Gladys Knight sang "God Bless America" during intermission, and boxing legend Michael Buffer belted out the starting lineups and a "Let's get ready to rumble" prior to puck drop.

So, yes, the stars were shining bright in Las Vegas.

But on the ice it wasn't the stars who factored into the outcome of the monumental game . NHL leading goal-scorer Alex Ovechkin was mostly silent with only two shots on goal for Washington, and Marc-Andre Fleury had a forgettable night allowing four goals for Vegas.

Instead, it was the Golden Knights' always under-appreciated fourth line that won the game, scoring three goals in the third period to power Vegas to a 6-4 victory and a 1-0 lead in the Stanley Cup Final.

Tomas Nosek scored the eventual game-winning goal to give the Golden Knights a 5-4 lead with 10:16 to play, then finished the Capitals off with an empty net goal in the final seconds.

"They are warriors for us and they got rewarded tonight," Vegas coach Gerard Gallant said. "It's great when you see those guys get rewarded. They're a big part of our group and you guys all know that. It's nice to see those guys chip in with a few goals."

Despite scoring only seven goals on the season, Nosek's play has been vital to Vegas' success. Whether it's providing important minutes on the fourth line, blocking shots in the defensive zone or killing penalties, he has done the thankless jobs required for a deep playoff run.

Now, on hockey's biggest stage, Nosek made the spectacular plays that everyone noticed.

"It's awesome to see," Vegas first-line winger Jonathan Marchessault said. "Those guys on the fourth line don't get enough credit. They work hard — probably work the hardest. They play well, play the right way and they don't get as much ice time as they want but they managed to get those big goals for us and that says a lot about our team."

Shea Theodore made a great play on Nosek's game-winner, holding the puck in the zone after his original shot deflected off a defender's leg. Theodore skated into the faceoff circle, found Nosek waiting on the backdoor and Nosek one-timed the puck past Washington goalie Braden Holtby.

Ryan Reaves (75) celebrates his crucial, game-tying goal with teammate Pierre-Edouard Bellemare during the third period of Game 1 in Las Vegas. (Las Vegas Sun)

"It's a great feeling," Nosek said. "You play in the Stanley Cup Final maybe once in your life so you try to enjoy it. I think every kid who is playing hockey dreams about scoring in the Stanley Cup Final, or winning it. I'm just happy the goal helped the team win the game."

But even in a two goal performance, Nosek's best play of the night was of the workman variety.

Nursing a one-goal lead in the final minute, the Golden Knights were desperately trying to hold on as the Capitals applied pressure with an extra attacker after pulling the goalie.

The puck was pushed back to Ovechkin for a one-timed slap shot, but Nosek dove in front of the man who recently won the NHL's hardest shot competition and got his stick on the puck. He immediately leaped to his skates and hustled down the ice to collect the puck and put it into the empty goal mouth.

"I felt good for him because he's a guy that works hard every game," fellow fourth-line forward Pierre-Edouard Bellemare said. "It's been an easy year for me to play with him, and sometimes we don't create a lot of offense but tonight it bounced right for us. It's nothing magical we did, or a crazy recipe. We are just trying to outwork whoever we're playing against and tonight we got rewarded."

The goals were only Nosek's second and third playoff goals of his career.

"The so-called fourth line went out there and battled hard," Gallant said. "They got pucks below the goal line and that's how you score goals. In a tight series when teams are blocking shots, big (Ryan Reaves) goes hard to the net, Nosek makes plays to the net and Bellemare competed hard."

It was Reaves who scored the game-tying goal early in the third. Vegas fell behind for the first time in the game, 4-3, and the momentum seemed to be tilting towards the Capitals. Then Reaves shoved his defender to the ice in front of the Washington goal, received the puck and lifted it top shelf.

It was Reaves' second spectacular goal in as many games. He had scored only one playoff goal in the 41 postseason games prior.

"I'm just trying to enjoy the ride," he said. "You don't get to this position very often in your career, so we have to enjoy it. I love this group. I love every guy on this team from the owner down to everybody."

Reaves was certainly enjoying the moment, even caught singing along with the in-arena music at one point.

"I'm always having fun. I love this game and you can't play it forever so you have to have fun while you're doing it. If you showed me more you'd see me singing a lot more."

Reaves has given the cameras more reason to focus on him lately, trading his former enforcer role for one that fits with Vegas' style of play. He has yet to drop the gloves as a Golden Knight, including Monday night when Washington bruiser Tom Wilson took Marchessault out of the game momentarily with a late blindside hit.

Many assumed a fight with Reaves would soon follow, but he was too occupied scoring game-changing goals to bother with a scrap.

For all of the glitz and glamour of Las Vegas — including the insanely long and masterfully choreographed pregame festivities — the Golden Knights have won this year by outworking teams.

The only difference, is now they're doing it in front of the entire hockey world.

In the locker room following the game a reporter asked Bellemare why the world is just now discovering Nosek.

"Because you aren't watching enough hockey, I guess," Bellemare replied with a smile. ■

Tomas Nosek and the Golden Knights' fourth line were essential playmakers in the Game 1 victory. (Las Vegas Sun)

BUCKLE UP

Series Tied After Golden Knights' Atypical Midgame Collapse
By Case Keefer

The fan experience of the NHL Playoffs is supposed to resemble the world's most frightening haunted house, with long stretches of shriek-inducing horror followed by only brief moments of respite. Vegas Golden Knights fans have lived a charmed existence by avoiding the hockey equivalent of a crazed masked man chasing them through hallways in the team's inaugural (post)season. They've enjoyed something more akin to a vacation at an all-inclusive tropical resort as the Golden Knights went 13-3 through the Game 1 of the Stanley Cup Final to shield fans from nearly any care in the hockey world.

That ended with a 3-2 loss to the Washington Capitals in Game 2 Wednesday night at T-Mobile Arena to even the Stanley Cup Final at 1-1. It's time to jump out of the hammock and prepare for a hacksaw.

This series is going to produce heart-pounding scares around every corner.

Let's start the startling with this: Game 2 winners have gone on to hoist the cup 74 percent of the time since the NHL expanded the championship series to a best–of–seven.

That doesn't mean Washington will walk to its franchise's first title, but it's easy to envision the Capitals having many of the same advantages of its forbearers.

They appeared to figure out the Golden Knights on Wednesday. Vegas' only other playoff loss at home came in the controversial 3-2 double-overtime setback in Game 2 of the Western Conference semifinal series against San Jose.

The Golden Knights' other pair of postseason defeats weren't pretty — a 4-2 defeat in Winnipeg in Game 1 of the Western Conference final and a 4-0 blowout at San Jose in Game 4 — but some solace was attached to each. Vegas improved as the game progressed against Winnipeg, a team that seemed spurred by an early wave of emotion stemming from the city's first-ever conference final appearance.

Even the San Jose blowout felt less alarming, with the promise of Vegas coming home after splitting the pair of road games. The pressure is firmly on the Golden Knights now, however, with the Stanley Cup Final shifting to Washington for Game 3 on Saturday and Game 4 on Monday.

They won't stand much of a chance if they play like they did for most of Wednesday's midgame.

And all of this on a night when Vegas had an opportunity to take a commanding lead and become the sixth team in NHL history to win 14 of the first 17 games in a single postseason.

It's hard to think that was the same Golden Knights team as the one that stumbled in so many areas for a 20-minute stretch between the first and second periods in Game 2. Goalie Marc-Andre Fleury couldn't make up for shortcomings elsewhere as he has so often in the postseason, with all three Washington goals coming during the span.

Alex Ovechkin's second-period power play goal gave the Washington Capitals a lead they would not relinquish. Lars Eller and Brooks Orpik also contributed goals for the Capitals in Game 2. (Las Vegas Sun)

Fleury can't be blamed for Alexander Ovechkin blasting his first goal of the series on a second-period power play, but he could have made a better play on the other two scores. That includes a weak Brooks Orpik wrister, which in fairness deflected off a player and then the post, that broke a personal 220-game goal-less drought.

Fleury, however, was not the primary problem.

He made two diving saves to atone for defensive lapses that were all too frequent. Vegas' offense joined in on the uncharacteristic showing.

Although the Golden Knights held a shots-on-goal edge through two periods, any heat map or shot chart revealed the Capitals as the team getting the more quality opportunities.

That's enough with the doom and gloom, though.

Here's a place to take a breath: Only once in the last 32 years has the lower-seeded team gone on to win the Stanley Cup Final when the series is tied 1-1.

Vegas did demonstrate some of its comeback mentality when Shea Theodore converted a power-play right before the second intermission to make the score 3-2.

The Golden Knights continued to attack in the third period — other than disastrously underperforming with more than a minute of 5-on-3 play — but Capitals goalie Braden Holtby made several big saves.

Vegas has answered adversity spectacularly all season. There's no reason to doubt the Golden Knights can do it again. There's no reason to think they can't win the series.

Game 2 just ensured the path to victory won't be a breeze this time; it's looking a lot more menacing. ∎

HARD KNOCKS

Vegas Golden Knights Look to Rebound from Game 3 Loss
By Jesse Granger

For some, this could be the opportunity to doubt the Vegas Golden Knights.

They have lost consecutive games in the Stanley Cup Final to the Capitals, who grabbed a 2-1 series advantage with a 3-1 victory on Saturday in Game 3. Washington, which has completely taken Vegas out of its fast-paced style of play, is now a minus-210 betting favorite to hoist Lord Stanley's Cup.

But as the first-year Golden Knights have shown all season, they play their best when outsiders count them out. There is still plenty of hockey left, players say.

"It's been said all year," forward James Neal said. "We know what we have in this room and we stick together. We got each other, we'll pick each other up focus on the next one. We'll have our best game of the year and tie it up."

The feeling after Saturday's game was eerily similar to two weeks ago in Winnipeg. The Jets pounded Vegas 4-2 in the opening game of the Western Conference Finals and the general consensus was the Golden Knights had finally met their match.

That was far from the case, as Vegas won the next four games in impressive fashion to become the first expansion team to reach the finals.

When Neal says the team will have its best game of the year, it's not just wishful thinking. He truly believes it, and to this point, there isn't a reason not to. After Vegas was blown out in Winnipeg, Jonathan Marchessault said

Game 2 was a must-win, and that they would show what type of team they are.

He went out and scored two goals and the Golden Knights dismantled Winnipeg in front of its home crowd.

The Golden Knights will have to do the same thing on Monday in Game 4 against Washington if they want to even the Stanley Cup Finals and steal back home ice advantage as the series shifts back to Las Vegas.

"We have what it takes," Vegas' Cody Eakin said. "It's going to come from within the locker room and within each other. We are still a confident group. It's one game and we are going to look to be a little better."

The Capitals have improved in each game this series while the Golden Knights have remained stagnant, and that has been the difference. The Caps' Alex Ovechkin has played like the superstar he is, and delivered for his team when they needed it most while Vegas' stars have been mostly a non-factor.

"We're still underdogs against them," Vegas; David Perron said. "They're a great team over there. Now the pressure is on them to keep going. We're going to find a way to answer. We're going to talk about it. It's tough tonight. Hurts a lot. But we gotta find a way to turn the page and it'll be better."

It's something coach Gerard Gallant has preached all season.

"You forget about tonight's game and get ready for

Alex Ovechkin (8) scores during the second period over Golden Knights defenseman Brayden McNabb and past goalie Marc-Andre Fleury. (AP Photo)

the next one," Gallant said. "They were the better team, they deserved to win and we move on."

Washington's forecheck has given the Golden Knights major problems, forcing turnovers, such as the one that Shea Theodore coughed up in the third period that led to the game-icing goal by Devante Smith-Pelly.

"Once we get it we have to have some poise with the puck, make the right play and make it easier on each other," Neal said. "Once we make a play we are rushing the next one, and vice versa. We have to have some poise, settle down a little bit and get back to what has made us successful."

Vegas has plenty of room for improvement. It's gotten next to nothing from the best line in hockey

(Marchessault, Reilly Smith and William Karlsson) and Marc-Andre Fleury appears to be rounding back into his superstar form after a slow start to the series.

It's commonly said that the Stanley Cup is the toughest trophy to win in all of sports. It takes 16 wins over the stretch of two months. To this point Vegas has breezed through the playoffs, making it look almost too easy at times.

But that's not the case with this series.

"Nothing's going to be given, we have to work for everything we get," Neal said. "It's so hard to win. It's so hard to get to this position. It's so hard to do anything. We recognize that. It's going to be a long series and we knew that right from the get go." ∎

NO ROOM FOR ERROR

Missed Opportunities Leave Golden Knights with Backs Against the Wall

By Jesse Granger

When James Neal's shot at a wide-open net rang off the far-side goal post and out of harm's way, it was as uplifting for the Washington Capitals as it was deflating for the Golden Knights.

"It probably changes the game," Neal said. "It's probably a different game after that. We get the first one. It's tough ... I had a wide-open net, and then I just hit the post. Definitely one I want to have back."

The Golden Knights controlled play early in Game 4, but after Neal's misfire the Capitals scored on three of the next seven shots and never looked back. Washington claimed a 6-2 win Monday night at Capital One Arena to take a 3-1 series lead, and push Vegas to the brink of elimination.

"It's do or die for us — we have no option," Neal said. "We have to figure out how to put the puck in the net, and we have to do it early. Work for our bounces, and hopefully they go our way, and we'll continue to play the right way. But just a few plays that we let up on and they're in the back of our net. But for the most part, I thought we were going."

Most Vegas players felt it was their best performance of the series, even better than their only win in Game 1. The numbers back them up, where the Golden Knights outshot Washington 30-23 and had a 53-28 CORSI advantage.

"It was frustrating because of the score," coach Gerard Gallant said. "I thought we played our best period of the final so far. We had two posts, had some good chances and we got nothing out of it. After the first period we came in there and said, 'Let's keep going, let's keep working hard and keep playing well because things can change in a hurry.'"

The Capitals trudged back to their locker room with a commanding 3-0 lead despite being outplayed and outchanced. Vegas had 13 scoring chances in the first 20 minutes compared with only three for Washington.

Many attribute the hot start for Washington to "puck luck," but Gallant disagrees.

"I heard that last series against us," he said. "People were saying that and you don't make excuses. You work hard and (play) your game, and I think tonight's game is a step forward for our group. When you work hard you're going to get those pucks to go in for you."

The players agree with Gallant, believing they need to play better and the bounces will go their way.

"You work for your bounces," Neal said. "There are definitely some plays there that were really close to going on, gone off a couple of skates or (goaltender Braden) Holtby just got a piece of it, a couple of open nets that we just missed, posts. We're right there, but at the end of the day you have to bury them. No feeling sorry for ourselves, we have to regroup, and like I said if

Vegas fans packed T-Mobile arena to watch a broadcast of Game 4 from Washington and cheer on their team. (AP Photo)

we play that way again we'll be just fine."

The Golden Knights aren't done, but they have run out of room for error. Down 3-1, the next loss will be their last this season.

"We've been good at regrouping," Neal said. "We have to play the same way and then bear down when we have those chances ... Go home, win one game, and the pressure is on them."

In the history of the Stanley Cup Final, teams that take a 3-1 lead are 32-1. The only team to come back from such a deficit was the 1942 Toronto Maple Leafs 76 years ago.

Still, if the Golden Knights can get a win in Game 5 Wednesday night at T-Mobile Arena it could start to creep into the minds of the Capitals. They've blown

more 3-1 series leads than any other team in the history of major pro sports with five, and are only 2-for-4 when holding a 3-1 series lead since Alex Ovechkin joined the team in 2005.

The pumpkin stem may be protruding through the roof of the Golden Knights' carriage, and the paint slowly turning orange, but if anyone can keep this Cinderella run alive, it's the team that's ripped through every record book they've come across.

Do the Golden Knights have any magic left?

"I hope so," Marc-Andre Fleury said. "Like I said, nobody's quitting. We're going home, we've had some success there. We just have to focus one period at a time, you know? Don't think too far ahead. Just play our game and see where that takes us." ■

NOT WITHOUT A FIGHT

Golden Knights Go Out Valiantly in Stanley Cup Loss to Capitals
By Case Keefer

Alex Tuch skated away from the melee-inflicted dog pile that followed a goal he orchestrated and toward the penalty box nodding his head.

The message was as sharp as the blade on the stick he left behind: Tuch's Golden Knights weren't intimidated by the Capitals in Game 5 of the Stanley Cup Final. Despite a series that had turned against them in so many ways, they would concede nothing.

Vegas played with that kind of an edge throughout Thursday night's elimination game, but unfortunately for Tuch and his teammates, it wasn't enough. Washington was able to do what its franchise had failed to do so often throughout its 44-year history and win a closeout game.

Capitals 4, Golden Knights 3.

The nation's capital finally has the championship it's excruciatingly sought for nearly 30 years. One of the greatest hockey players in the world, Alexander Ovechkin, finally has the crown he's chased for what feels like just as long.

Even the thousands of Golden Knights fans out of the 18,529 in attendance must have felt a trace of happiness for Ovechkin as he paraded the cup around the T-Mobile Arena ice. Not that the appreciation came anywhere close to overpowering the predominant feeling of Vegas fans — pain.

The chances for major professional sports titles simply don't come around very often. Just ask Washington.

Inaugural season or not, there's no soothing the sting of defeat after coming this close. Don't let anyone argue otherwise.

The city hasn't had a team long enough to know true torment? Try being blackballed from every attempt to lure any major professional sport for decades because of an archaic fallacy on the nature of the gaming industry.

But if there's any solace to be found for the suddenly hockey-crazed valley in the immediate aftermath of this loss, it should come in the way the Golden Knights fought. The Game 5 loss was far from the no-show seen so often from mentally broken teams in closeout games against an opponent that's dominated the series.

The Golden Knights showed plenty of flashes of why they've become so beloved.

For more than 30 minutes starting from the time Tuch assisted on a Reilly Smith power-play goal to make the score Vegas 3-2, it looked like the Golden Knights would extend the greatest expansion season in sports history.

They had just scored two goals in seven minutes, the first being what felt like the umpteenth time of the playoffs that they answered an opponent's score immediately. Less than three minutes after eventual Conn

The Vegas Golden Knights salute their home fans one last time to close out an unparalleled inaugural season. (Las Vegas Sun)

Smythe winner Ovechkin scored his 15th playoff goal and third of the Stanley Cup on a power play, David Perron deflected a Tomas Tatar shot in to tie the game at 2-2.

Unlike their Game 3 loss, the Golden Knights weren't struggling to find solid offensive chances. Unlike their Game 4 loss, Fleury hadn't ever seem flustered.

He sprawled out on multiple occasions in the first two periods to make stops reminiscent of those that helped deliver him to the Stanley Cup Final with the best playoff save percentage (.947) in history among goalies with at least 15 games.

Alas, Fleury could neither counteract shoddy defense on a tying-goal from Devante Smith-Pelly with 10 minutes remaining nor prevent Lars Eller from getting behind him and poking in a rebound on the game-winner three minutes later.

But think of where Fleury, the Golden Knights' consummate leader, has brought them. It was almost exactly a year ago that he walked across a stage in the same arena as an expansion draft pick.

No one in the building thought he'd have the chance to give up a Stanley Cup-winning goal in virtually the same spot.

"The best first year any team has ever had," NHL Commissioner Gary Bettman reminded the crowd before awarding the Capitals the cup and turning boos into cheers.

A lot of that will always be attributed to Fleury, who again appeared to instill in the Golden Knights a winning attitude before the game that ended their season. In pregame warmups, Ovechkin playfully nicked Fleury's stick as he stretched.

Problem was, Fleury wasn't in a playful mood. He strode alongside Ovechkin down the center of the ice, and seemed to impart some choice words.

Later, Fleury returned the favor and tapped Ovechkin's shin pad. He had no intention of succumbing on Thursday night. The Golden Knights had no intention of succumbing.

The fight they showed won't cure the hurt, but the Golden Knights at least went out in a similar fashion to the way they spent the season — making Vegas proud. ■

Vegas Golden Knights and Washington Capitals players shake hands following the Capitals' decisive Game 5 victory. (Las Vegas Sun)

ALL THE PIECES MATTER

One Defining Moment from Every Golden Knights Contributor

By Jesse Granger • June 2, 2018

Brayden McNabb, #3, Defenseman

The Los Angeles Kings left McNabb exposed in the expansion draft last June, and he ended their season in April. McNabb clinched the Golden Knights' first-round playoff sweep over the Kings with a second-period goal in a 1-0 Game 4 victory.

Deryk Engelland, #5, Defenseman

Engelland, a Las Vegas resident for more than a decade, had a dream season on the ice while setting career highs in nearly every stat. Still, nothing will top the speech he gave before the October 10 home opener, just nine days after the mass shooting on the Las Vegas Strip. "To the families and friends of the victims, we'll do everything we can to help you and our city heal. We are Vegas Strong," Engelland said.

Colin Miller, #6, Defenseman

Miller has been the Golden Knights' best offensive defenseman all season. His best performance came on January 21 in a 5-1 win over the Carolina Hurricanes, when he scored the game-winning goal with a blistering slapshot and assisted on two other goals.

Jon Merrill, #15, Defenseman

Merrill doesn't score often, but when he does, they count. Four of his seven career goals have been game-winners, including his only one for the Golden Knights. He beat Pittsburgh's Matt Murray on December 14 at T-Mobile Arena to give Vegas a 2-1 win over the back-to-back Stanley Cup champion Penguins.

James Neal, #18, Left Wing

Neal scored the two goals that started it all for the Golden Knights this season. He netted the first one in franchise history to draw Vegas even with the Dallas Stars in the October 6 season opener, then flipped the puck over goalie Kari Lehtonen while sliding on his knees for the game winner.

Reilly Smith, #19, Right Wing

Most of Smith's highlight-reel plays this season have been assists, but he took matters into his own hands in his biggest moment. He raced down the ice in a 2-2 tie with Winnipeg in Game 4 of the Western Conference Finals, and fired shortside, past the goalie's blocker to give Vegas the win and a 3-1 series lead.

Cody Eakin, #21, Center

Midway through the year, the defensive-minded Eakin had fallen into a major offensive slump. He had registered only one goal and two points in 25 games before busting out with a two-goal, three point performance in a win over the Red Wings on March 8.

Oscar Lindberg, #24, Center

Early in the season, when almost no one believed the Golden Knights were legitimate, Lindberg was a big part of the team's hot start. The former Ranger scored four goals in a nine-game span in October to help Vegas to its early 8-1 start.

Erik Haula (56) and David Perron (57) are congratulated by Golden Knights teammates after scoring during Game 5 against the Sharks. (Las Vegas Sun)

Shea Theodore, #27, Defenseman

On Dec. 20, with the Golden Knights and Tampa Bay Lightning tied 3-3 and the final seconds ticking away, the puck emerged from a scrum behind the Lightning net, right to the stick of Theodore. He blasted the shot past Andrei Vasilevskiy with just 2.3 seconds left to give the Knights a walk-off win over the league's top team.

William Carrier, #28, Left Wing

Carrier set the tone for the postseason run with 21 hits in Vegas' first two playoff games, a pair of wins over the Kings. He finished fifth on the Golden Knights with 113 hits this season despite playing in only 37 games.

Marc-Andre Fleury, #29, Goaltender

It's nearly impossible to whittle Fleury's season down to one moment. He's carried the team all year, shattering postseason records in the process. But the back-to-back diving saves he made against the Jets' Mark Scheifele to preserve a win in Game 3 of the Western Conference Finals have been as important as any sequence this season.

Malcolm Subban, #30, Goaltender

Two years after using a first-round pick on Subban, the Boston Bruins waived him from their roster. The Golden Knights claimed him, and he revived his career with a 13-

4-2 record for Vegas this season, including a spectacular shootout win December 8 in Nashville (a squad that features his older brother P.K.) in which he made 41 saves and shut the Predators out in six shootout attempts.

Maxime Lagace, #33, Goaltender

After early-season injuries struck Fleury, Subban and Oscar Dansk, fourth-string goalie Lagace was thrust into the first NHL action of his career. The youngster kept the Golden Knights afloat while the others recovered, including a stretch from November 16 to December 9 in which Vegas went 5-1 with Lagace in net

Ryan Carpenter, #40, Left Wing

Like many Golden Knights this season, Carpenter starred against his former team. Waived by the Sharks earlier in the season, Carpenter set up an empty-net goal by Eakin to end San Jose's playoff run in Game 6 of the Western Conference semifinals.

Pierre-Edouard Bellemare, #41, Center

In the middle of the second period during Vegas' 4-1 win over the Avalanche on March 26, Bellemare was crawling across the ice with blood pouring from his face after taking a slap shot beneath his left eye. He returned to the game without missing a shift. Bellemare's toughness has been critical for Golden Knights on the ice and in the locker room.

Luca Sbisa, #47, Defenseman

Sbisa spent a large portion of the season on the injured reserve, but early in the year he helped establish the Knights as one of the better defensive teams in the NHL. He was matched up with the opposing team's best players on a nightly basis and held his own, which has continued into the playoffs.

Erik Haula, #56, Center

As the clock ticked closer to midnight on April 13, Haula finally ended the longest game in Golden Knights' franchise history. Haula streaked into the Kings' zone, deked goaltender Jonathan Quick and slid the puck under him for a double-overtime winner to give Vegas a 2-0 lead in the first-round series.

David Perron, #57, Right Wing

Perron racked up 66 points and four game-winning goals for Vegas this season, but the numbers pale in comparison to his leadership in the locker room. As he wrote in his piece for The Players Tribune, "Every guy in our room has a chip on his shoulder. And every time we step on the ice it's a fight to prove our worth. That was clear from first time we put the Knight over our chests."

William Karlsson, #71, Center

"Wild Bill" had many memorable moments, from his a pair of hat tricks, to a playoff overtime game-winner in San Jose, but his March 31 goal against the Sharks was the stuff of Vegas legend. Karlsson went between the legs before beating Martin Jones with a shorthanded goal to clinch the Pacific Division Title for the Golden Knights.

Ryan Reaves, #75, Right Wing

It took him more than 200 minutes of ice time with Vegas to net his first goal, but he couldn't have picked a better time for the breakthrough. The Winnipeg native tipped Luca Sbisa's point shot past Jets' goalie Connor Hellebuyck to give Vegas a 2-1 win in Game 5, punching the team's ticket to the Stanley Cup Final.

Brad Hunt, #77, Defenseman

Hunt spent much of the season as a healthy scratch, but that didn't stop him from bringing a fun-loving attitude and nonstop energy to the locker room. He earned a nomination for the Masterton Trophy, given to the NHL player who best exemplifies perseverance, sportsmanship and dedication to hockey.

Jonathan Marchessault, #81, Left Wing

Never shy around microphones, Marchessault made it crystal clear the Golden Knights needed to win Game 2 of the conference finals after a loss in Game 1, calling it a "must-win." He responded with two clutch goals to lead Vegas to victory.

The Vegas Golden Knights celebrate their 3-2 win over the Winnipeg Jets in Game 4 of Western Conference Finals. (Las Vegas Sun)

Nate Schmidt, #88, Defenseman

In the Golden Knights' double-overtime win over the Kings in the first round of the playoffs, Schmidt led all Vegas skaters in ice time. He emerged as a No. 1 defender this season, and proved it once again on April 13, blocking three shots during his 51 shifts that totaled an mammoth 37:18 of time without yielding a single goal while on the ice.

Alex Tuch, #89, Right Wing

From not being in possession of a locker when the season started—and having to sit on a fold-out chair in the Golden Knights locker room—to blossoming into one of the leading scorers in the playoffs. Tuch showed his growth in the crucial Game 5 of against San Jose with two goals, including a gorgeous tip past Martin Jones from just in front of the crease.

Tomas Tatar, #90, Left Wing

He faced pressure as general manager George McPhee's big trade-deadline acquisition but struggled to find a place in the lineup. After sitting out multiple games, Tatar was given a chance and cashed in with a momentum-swinging goal in Game 2 of the conference finals in Winnipeg.

Tomas Nosek, #92, Left Wing

Nosek is known as one of the Golden Knights' most trustworthy forwards and one of Gallant's most trusted penalty killers. He also etched his name into the team's playoff roll by scoring the winning goal in Game 4 versus Winnipeg, atoning for a penalty moments earlier that set up a tying power-play goal by the Jets. ∎

IN CLOSING

Knights More Than Filled Las Vegas' Cup
By Brian Greenspun • June 8, 2018

Oh, what a night.

Our first hockey season didn't end as we hoped, but the final game showed all the fight and passion that the Vegas Golden Knights are celebrated for worldwide. But, then again, who in Las Vegas dared to even dream of such things when the Knights took to the ice in their regular-season home opener last Oct. 10?

It took some brilliant minds to realize that Las Vegas could be a hockey town. And it took thousands of hockey-hungry fans to show their support through season ticket purchases well in advance of the first puck drop. But hockey happened.

And with the tragedy of Oct. 1 casting a pall over our city, how could we even think about anything as frivolous as the opening night of a brand new hockey adventure? And yet, it couldn't have come at a better time.

Who would have thought it would be the Vegas Golden Knights? But, they were here, they were ours and we, a million fans in Las Vegas and millions around the world, were theirs. It was an instant love affair that was somewhat reminiscent of the way Las Vegas grew to love the UNLV Runnin' Rebels back in the day when a national championship was just a dream.

You couldn't go anywhere in this country without someone talking about the Rebels. Likewise, I couldn't go anywhere this past year — especially to places that knew hockey — without people talking about the Golden Knights. When I was in Washington, D.C., last week the hotel was flying two flags at the front door. One was for the Capitals and the other — hanging with equal prominence — was for the Golden Knights.

When the game was over and the fate of the Stanley Cup was sealed, what impressed me most is that the fans didn't file out. They stayed at their seats in T-Mobile Arena. Perhaps it was because they had never seen a Stanley Cup presentation or perhaps they just wanted to show their immense gratitude for the team that had captured our hearts and imagination. It was probably both — and more.

What it showed to the world, though, was a city that has grown into its own as a place where professional sports are welcome, appreciated and supported. And when the Golden Knights stayed on the ice to recognize the fans in attendance, to thank them for believing that miracles really can happen, they sealed the deal.

It took Washington 44 years to finally win a Stanley Cup, so we shouldn't begrudge them their well-earned victory. Neither can we dismiss the unbelievable run at

Las Vegas Sun

the Cup that the Golden Knights made in just their first season. It was truly breathtaking.

Bill Foley, together with the Maloof family, led the effort to bring major-league hockey to Las Vegas, and they were joined by the thousands of fans who bought season tickets in advance of a season they could never have imagined. They found a home at T-Mobile and set records that may never be broken. And, along the way, they gave us all a reason to come together to root for something good. Something fun. Something that could help turn tragedy into something…else… Something glorious.

Las Vegas has its very own hockey team. And, one day soon, it will have its very own place on the Stanley Cup.

Thanks, Golden Knights, for these memories and all those to come. ◼